UNIX
Training Guide

UNIX
Training Guide

Clifford Mould

Pitman

PITMAN PUBLISHING
128 Long Acre, London, WC2E 9AN

A Division of Longman Group UK Limited

© Clifford Mould 1991

First published in Great Britain 1991

British Library Cataloguing in Publication Data
Mould, Clifford
   Unix training guide.
   I. Title
   005.4

ISBN 0–273–03421–9

Typeset by ⋀ Tek Art Ltd, Addiscombe, Croydon, Surrey

Printed and bound in Great Britain

Contents

Section E Introduction to programming in UNIX   83

Introduction

The UNIX operating system has grown steadily both in its user-base and in popularity since its beginnings in the early 1970s. As the power of computers has increased in relation to size, multi-user systems at departmental and small company level have become a reality. Powerful desk-top UNIX workstations have also proliferated and the consequence of all these developments is that more and more computer users find themselves working in a UNIX environment.

There are a number of other disk operating systems, such as MS–DOS and OS/2. MS–DOS and OS/2, developed by Microsoft for use on IBM compatible personal computers, enable a single user workstation environment. UNIX enables multi-tasking, multi-user information processing. The new generation of powerful RISC architecture workstations can provide user-friendly graphical interfaces like X-windows. PCs can also be used as terminals to a UNIX system and when these or dedicated UNIX workstations are connected to a central UNIX file-server, a distributed system is created that can handle the total information processing requirements of most organisations.

This *Guide* is intended to help new users to become familiar with UNIX operating system commands and to give an introduction to simple programming techniques that can process information without the expense of applications software both in financial terms and also in processing overheads.

The book does not attempt to provide an exhaustive or detailed description of every command. Rather, it gives practical examples of UNIX commands that will enable users to have both the confidence to look after their files and also a firm foundation upon which to build, should they wish to go further.

Note to system administrators

The *Guide* assumes that users will log in for the first time with an open user id and it will then show them how to set up their own passwords. They should have full access to their home directory area so that they can create and update files and directories. It is hoped that users would have read-only access to the system directories such as /bin, /dev and /etc. System administration commands have not been covered, nor have commands such as **cpio** and **tar** which might involve removable media. Printing is kept to a minimum, except in Section C Task 19 where the scheduler is discussed. Unhanging a terminal using **ps** and **kill** are discussed in Appendix 3. It would be very useful if an open access directory called **/ascii** could be created to contain a selection of text files.

Background to UNIX

UNIX started life in the early 1970s at Bell Laboratories in the USA. The programming language 'C' was also developed there and by 1973 much of the operating system had been rewritten in 'C'. This was the first time that an operating system had been written in a high level computer language.

The advantage of this is that UNIX can be transported to any processor which has a C compiler. Only a very small part of the operating system would have to be specially written in the native assembly language of the processor. It is this **portability** of the UNIX system across the widest possible range of different computer hardware that has been the reason for its rapid growth in popularity.

The structure of UNIX

UNIX consists of two main parts which are always pictured like a nut with a central kernel surrounded by a shell.

The **kernel** controls:
- the central resources of the computer (memory, CPU)
- the sharing of resources between processes (concurrency)
- the peripheral systems (disks, terminals, printers)
- the organisation of the central filestore
- file security, access and process accounting

The **shell** represents the boundary with the outside world and provides:
- the user interface, or command processor
- utility programs, available to and adaptable by the user

Applications software

There is now a wide range of business, scientific, production, CAD/CAM and other software which runs under UNIX.

Probably the most typical applications are in the area of multi-user accounts systems which use between 8 and 32 terminals.

Office automation is the next most common application, where the emphasis is on:
- central data with easy file management
- security and access control
- integrated word processing, spreadsheet & database
- electronic mail
- scheduling meetings, diaries
- desk-top organisers

All these are provided by such software as the UNIPLEX integrated office automation suite of programs running under UNIX.

Using the keyboard with UNIX ▬▬▬▬▬

ENTER

Always press the ENTER key or (Return ↵) when you have finished typing a command. This tells UNIX to begin processing the command.

Computer keys and typewriter keys

Computers never use the lower-case letter **l** in place of numeric **1**. Be careful also to differentiate between a zero **0** and the upper-case letter **O**.

UNIX commands are **case sensitive**, that is to say upper-case and lower-case mean quite different things. Most UNIX commands are typed into the computer using lower-case characters.

Cursor control keys

The spacebar moves the cursor along to the right, one character at a time. The backspace ← key deletes characters as it moves the cursor to the left. The direction, or **arrow** keys are not normally used in UNIX command processing.

Control key combinations

The control key CTRL, located to the left of the keyboard, enables the transmission of special codes to the CPU. You must hold down the control key while you press another key, as you do when using the shift key. Control key combinations are written **Ctrl-D**, or sometimes **^D** or (Ctrl)+(d)

Key	Function	Explanation	DOS equivalent
ctrl-c	interrupt	exit or abort a process	identical
ctrl-d	end of file	finish entering text	same as ctrl-z
ctrl-u	kill current command line		same as ctrl-x
ctrl-s	suspend scrolling		identical
ctrl-q	continue scrolling		press any key
del	destructive backspace		identical
@	at the end of line aborts command		no equivalent

In a multi-user system with 'dumb' terminals, every keystroke goes to the CPU and then back to the VDU – this is called full duplex transmission. If the CPU is busy there may be a delay in echoing characters to the screen. If you are impatient, this may cause you problems!

Section A: The multi-user system ▰▰▰

A UNIX network is a true multi-user system as opposed to a standalone microcomputer, or even a PC network.

Where many people share common resources, especially storage devices, the security of the system becomes very important. Even if you are working at a single user UNIX workstation, your personal storage area needs to be kept safe from other users. Protection of a user's own file systems is provided by a number of facilities, beginning with the **login** procedure.

Task 1   Logging in and passwords

Objective

To access the system by logging in and identifying yourself by means of a password.

Instructions

To gain access to the system you must login. Before you can do this, the system administrator must first give you a **user identity** or '**id**', pronounced *eye dee*, e.g.

```
user1,  claudia, socstuds23 etc
```

A password should be associated with such an identity.

The combination of **id** and password can be used to control access to different areas of the file-store, as well as the permissions associated with the files themselves.

Activity 1.1

Logging on to the system

Your terminal should display the login prompt:

```
login:
```

If it does not, make sure the terminal is switched on then press the `ENTER` or `Return ↵` key to wake it up (start it working).

Type your user **id** and press `ENTER`.

Always use lowercase letters in UNIX.

UNIX **ids** can be up to 8 characters long and may include digits e.g.

```
e.g.  user1, user2, user3, joe,  guest
```

The system manager's id is usually called **root**.

You will not be asked for a password the first time you log on to the system. An initial user id is normally issued to you as an '**open id**'.

Activity 1.2

Making or changing your password

Passwords can be changed by users at any time by typing the command:

```
passwd    ENTER

changing password for [user]
New password:
```

Enter your new password

```
Re-enter new password:
```

Enter it again

Because the password is not echoed to the screen you need to type it in twice to be absolutely certain.

Now log off by typing the command **exit**, i.e.

```
$ exit
```

Log in again, mistype your new password to see what happens, then log in again correctly.

You should always log off before finishing a session or switching off a terminal. Failure to do this could compromise the security of the system.

Instructions

Terminal characteristics

One of the problems people encounter with UNIX is that it is not considered to be user-friendly in its raw form. This is because it does not make assumptions about the terminal you may be working on, nor the kind of environment you prefer.

The terminal may be a long way from the CPU, even at the other end of a telephone link, so data has to be transmitted serially.

The direct access to screen drivers which we enjoy on IBM PC family and compatibles is not possible except on a directly driven UNIX workstation with its own CPU, or over a high speed network link using, say, fibre-optic connections.

Key words

id
password

Task 2

Who else is logged in?

Objectives

To see who is logged in.
To remind yourself of your current login identity.
To see which terminal you are using.

Instructions

The **who** command

The UNIX prompt is a dollar sign **$**. When the $ prompt is displayed it means that the computer is waiting for you to enter a UNIX command.

In this guide therefore, the dollar sign is a signal to you to type the command that follows. **Do not type the dollar sign**, but end the command with the ENTER or Return ↵ key.

Examples of typical responses that you should get from the computer usually follow on the next line of the page. Do not attempt to type in anything from a line beginning with e.g. unless specifically told to do so.

Activity 2.1

To see who else is on the system, type:

```
$ who
```

e.g:

ID	Terminal name	Date	Time
user1	tty2	25 Nov	13:56
root	tty0	25 Nov	08:30

In case you cannot remember your identity, type:

```
$ who am i
```

e.g. accounts3   tty7   12 Feb 19.15

The who command has a number of options controlled by **switches** that come after the command. In UNIX, switches are preceded by the minus '−' sign.

switch	meaning
-u	'useful' additional information
-a	all possible information
-l	lisfs those ttys that are not logged on and which ports are therefore free.

```
$ who -u
```

To see a complete list of switches, type:

```
$ who -z
```

Activity 2.2	The tty command

tty is an abbreviation of 'teletype', which was the original name for a remote terminal.

The tty command tells you the number of the terminal that issued the tty command.

```
$ tty
```

e.g. `/dev/tty7`

/dev refers to the /dev subdirectory that stores information relating to devices such as terminals and printers.

Each terminal on a UNIX system has a unique number to identify it. Sometimes it is useful to know what the number of your terminal is. It is also useful to know where different users are logged in. Programs in the UNIX environment are often referred to as 'processes' and they belong to users who 'run' or 'execute' them at a terminal.

Find out for yourself if there any switches that can be used with tty.

Note: If a program has a problem or 'hangs up', the user or system administrator will need to know the tty number in order to identify the offending process before trying to clear the terminal.

Key words	**who**
	who am i
	tty
	switch
	/dev

Task 3

Sending direct messages

Objective

To communicate directly with another user who is logged in at another terminal.

Instructions

If you are working at a terminal which is part of a multi-user network, you can send messages directly to other users who are currently logged on to the system.

Activity 3.1

Using the write command

To send a message *directly* to another user, type the command **write** followed by the user identity of the person you want to write to, e.g.

```
$ write jackie
```

It is always a good idea to use **who** because you can only **write** to someone who is currently logged on, and you have to know their identity exactly.

```
$ who
```

ID	Terminal		Date	
user3	tty4		15 Oct	12:33
root	tty0		15 Oct	14:05
jackie	tty2		15 Oct	14:12

```
$ write jackie
```

[type in your message; each line is sent when you press ENTER] (shown as Return ↵) e.g.

```
I thought we were supposed to be meeting at 2.15? Return ↵
See you in Room 45 in five minutes, OK?! Return ↵
Ctrl+d
```

[end the message with **ctrl-d**, the end-of-file marker]

The recipient will hear a bleep and the screen will display something like this:

```
Message from user3 on tty0 at [Thu Oct 25 10:26:51]...

I thought we were supposed to be meeting at 2.15?
See you in room 45 in five minutes, OK?!
<EOT>
```

<EOT> stands for end of transmission, so you know that the message is over.

As soon as you receive a **write** message you can return your own message to the originator, e.g:

```
$ write user3

Sorry Jane, someone on the phone went on a bit...
Return ↵ Can we make it 3.00? Ctrl+d
```

You do not have to wait for the <EOT> sign, but a simultaneous two-way conversation can get confusing.

Receiving longer messages via **write** can be frustrating for the recipient unless you are a quick typist. One way to do this is to type the message into a file then transmit the file in one burst of concise prose. This will be explained in Task 17.

If you do not wish to have your work interrupted by a direct message, it is possible to disable the reception of such messages by typing:

```
$ mesg n
```

When you want to receive incoming messages again, type

```
$ mesg y
```

If you attempt to write to a user who has disable reception of direct messages, UNIX will tell you:

```
Permission denied.
```

Activity 3.2

Broadcasting messages via the wall command

To send a message to everyone who is currently logged on to the system you can use the command **wall** which stands for 'write all'.

Normally this command is used by the system administrator to warn users that the system is about to be taken down for maintenance. You may find that you do not have the authority to use this command as it can be very irritating if overused.

This is an example of what you might do:

```
$ wall
```

Type in your message; each line is sent when you press ENTER (shown as (Return ↵)) e.g.

```
Message to all members of sales team (Return ↵)
-from the Sales Director (Return ↵)

Urgent meeting re Friday's exhibition
4.30 p.m. in my office.  Be there!! (Return ↵)
(Ctrl)+(d)
```

[end the message with **ctrl-d**, the end-of-file marker]

Troubleshooting

If the commands do not work at all and you get a message like:

```
write: not found
```

it is probably because you have not been given permission to use the command(s).

The most obvious source of errors using **write** are:
- the receiving user is not logged on
- you misspelled or mistook their id
- you did not leave a space between the command and the id

Do not forget that with both the commands the message is not ended until you send the end-of-file marker **ctrl-d**. If you forget to do this your colleague at the receiving terminal will be kept waiting for you to finish the message.

write and **wall** must be used with care or else you could become an unpopular member of your UNIX fraternity.

Key words	**write**
	ctrl-d
	<EOT>
	wall

7

Task 4   Electronic mail

Objectives

To send and receive electronic mail messages.

Instructions

You will often want to leave a message or memorandum for a colleague who is not logged on or whose work you would not wish to interrupt with a direct message.

You can use the **mail** command to leave messages in a special and private area of the filestore reserved for each user. When users who have been left mail log on they are told by the system whether there are messages in their mailbox.

Activity 4.1

Sending a mail message

Using the **mail** command is very similar to using **write**. You need to know the **id** of the recipient. To test the whole process, try leaving yourself a message. Let's assume your id is jackie:

```
$ mail jackie
```

[type in the message, after the last line type **ctrl-d** to close the file]

The **id** of the sender and the date and time will automatically be included at the head of the message, e.g:

```
From jim Thu Oct 25 10:31 BST 1990

Please let me have your your regional sales
report by Friday 3.0p.m. at the latest.

Jim Ford
```

Send several short mail messages to your own user id so that you can practise using the command and also have some mail to deal with in the following activity.

Activity 4.2

Picking up mail

Now log off, by typing **exit** or **ctrl-d**. Ctrl-d will log you off because UNIX regards the keyboard as an open file! If you type the end-of-file marker at the $ prompt, UNIX considers this to be a signal to say that the keyboard file is closed and that no further dialogue is required, so it logs you off. Be careful how you use ctrl-d, press it only once at a time; if you find that you have been inadvertently logged off, this is probably because you have pressed it too many times!

When you log back on you should see the message

```
you have mail
```

You can ignore this if there are more pressing things to attend to, otherwise type

```
$ mail
```

The first item of mail will be displayed, followed by a question mark prompt. **mail** is waiting for you to tell it what to do next...

?   — press ENTER to leave the message to be read again later. Mail will display any further messages.

? d   — deletes the message if you no longer need it and exits from mail if there are no more messages.

? p   — prints the message again

? s   — stores the message in the file **mbox** in the user's home directory

? q   — quits the mail command

? x   — exits from mail without deleting or changing anything

You can send mail to a number of users by typing several names on the command line:

```
$ mail lloyd jackie fred saleem
```

It does not matter which terminal of a multi-user user system a user logs on to because mail is not *terminal dependant*.

You can use mail on a single-user UNIX workstation to leave messages for other users who will log on after you have finished your session.

Key word	mail

Task 5   **Time for UNIX**

Objectives   To display the date and time from the system clock.

Instructions   The system clock in the computer's CPU can be accessed by UNIX so that the current system date and time can be displayed. Whether this is accurate or even remotely correct depends on the system administrator, one of whose tasks is to check on such things and to reset the clock if there has been an interruption to the main power supply (heaven forbid!) or to adjust for Summer Time, for instance.

Activity 5.1   Displaying the current system date and time

To display both time and date, simply type the command

```
$ date
```

```
Mon Oct 22  08:45:12 BST 1990
```

UNIX displays time relative to GMT, and converts to local times such as BST, EDT etc.

Unlike DOS, UNIX does not invite the user to reset the clock whenever the date and time are displayed. Only the system administrator can normally do this. There is a UNIX command called time, but this is concerned with auditing the amount of time taken by the CPU to execute a program.

Having an accurate system clock is an essential feature of a multi-user system. Many processes are pre-programmed to run at certain times on certain days or dates. The UNIX operating system has to log the times when processes run, when users log on and off and so on because one of its key features is that it provides the framework for an **auditable** computer system.

Activity 5.2   The system calendar

You can easily get a neat display of the calendar for the current month just by typing

```
$ cal

      October 1990
Su Mo Tu We Th Fr Sa
    1  2  3  4  5  6
 7  8  9 10 11 12 13
14 15 16 17 18 19 20
21 22 23 24 25 26 27
28 29 30 31
```

To display calendar listings for a whole year, type

```
$ cal 1991
```

You can display a single month in a specified year by typing

```
$ cal 1 2000
```

```
        January 2000
Su Mo Tu We Th Fr Sa
                    1
 2  3  4  5  6  7  8
 9 10 11 12 13 14 15
16 17 18 19 20 21 22
23 24 25 26 27 28 29
30 31
```

Try to find out how far back the calendar goes. Or how far into the future?

There is another useful utility called **calendar** that provides an electronic diary and appointment system for users. When you have learned how to make a text file you will be shown how to use this powerful feature.

Key words	date
	cal

Getting help

Objectives   To use the **man** and **learn** commands to try to get help in UNIX.

Instructions   Whether or not help is available about the UNIX operating system and its commands
depends very much on what the system administrator decides should be available. In
many UNIX systems the main objective of the administrator is to confine users to
applications software and not to let them near the operating system at all.

'Help' files take up space on disk drives and if space is scarce, the commands below
may not be available to you.

There is no official UNIX command called **help**, which is unusual, as most software
programs have some sort of help feature. Try it out on your system:

```
$ help
```

e.g. `help? -you must be joking!`

Two officially helpful commands that may be available are **man** and **learn**

Activity 6.1   Using the manual method

The command **man** displays selected pages from the UNIX MANUAL, if it is on-line.
In this context **on-line** means that the file containing the manual is on a disk drive
currently connected to the CPU.

If you require information about the command *write*, for instance, type

```
$ man write
```

Documentation on each command is presented under at least three headings:
Name – gives the name of the command and a brief description of what it does
Synopsis – tells you the command **syntax**, including any other words or special
switches (see p. 3) that can be used on the command line
Description – gives a more detailed summary of its functions and how to use them.

Some commands have a section called **bugs** where any known bugs or
anomalies are listed.

Activity 6.2   Computer aided learning

You may find that the command **learn** is available on your system. Learn is
interactive and if you just type **learn** the program will ask you what you would like
to know more about.

Alternatively you can name a subject, such as

```
$ learn vi
```

This will provide instruction on how to use the visual editing program that comes with
nearly all versions of UNIX.

Key words   man
                      learn

Section B: The UNIX filestore

Task 7   Files and directories

Objectives

To understand the UNIX file system.

Instructions

Programs and data that are required permanently are stored as files which are identified by their respective filenames.

Files are grouped together and stored in **directories** in a similar way to that in which paper documents are categorised and put into folders, then placed in the various drawers of appropriate filing cabinets. The UNIX directory structure can be pictured (like the DOS directory structure) as an upside-down tree with the root at the top. The symbol for the **root directory is** the forward-slash **/** (unlike DOS which uses the back-slash symbol ****).

A typical UNIX filestore will be organised into a tree structure looking something like this:

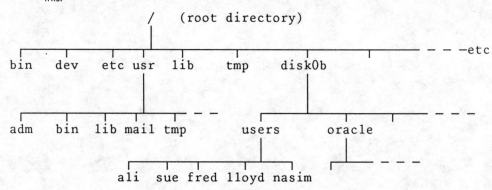

Note that there can be several directories with the same name, such as lib and tmp. Most of the first level directories will have a considerable sub-directory structure below them. I have shown only a small part of the tree; you will soon explore your own directory structure and perhaps draw a map of it.

Activity 7.1

Finding your bearings

When you login to a UNIX system, you are assigned to a **home** directory. Assuming that you have not yet moved away from this home directory, find out what it is called by typing:

```
$ pwd
```

e.g. `/disk0b/users/nasim`

The command **pwd** prints the working directory on to the screen so that you know where you are. You cannot display the current or working directory within the prompt as you can in DOS, so you need to get into the habit of using **pwd** regularly.

Now move to the root directory by typing

```
$ cd /

$ pwd

/
```

You can get back to your home directory by typing the cd command with no parameter.

```
$ cd

$ pwd

disk0b/users/nasim
```

You will easily remember the command **cd** because it stands for **c**hange **d**irectory. The general form of the command is:

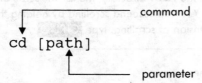

```
cd [path]
```
parameter

```
cd  /usr/adm
```
there is always a space between the command and the parameter(s)

When a UNIX command is described, words enclosed in square brackets like [path] refer to parameters which may be optional. You have to substitute a parameter of the type defined. Note that you do not type the brackets, i.e.

```
$ cd /usr/lib
```

/users/lib is called a **path**. It shows the path from the root directory '**/**' to the directory 'lib' via the directory 'usr'. Because the UNIX directory tree is quite large some path names can be long, for instance /usr/lib/terminfo/icl

Troubleshooting   Be prepared for the following error messages:

```
cd\: not found
```
— you have used the DOS *backslash* instead of the UNIX *forward* slash

```
cd/: not found
```
— you did not leave a space between **cd** and **/**

```
cd/usr/adm: cannot execute
```
— as above

```
/user/adm: bad directory
```
— the directory is *usr* with no e

15

Activity 7.2	Listing files within the directories

Change to your home directory:

```
$ cd
```

See if there are any files there by typing the command **ls**

```
$ ls
```

If there are no files there, change directory to **/bin**, there will be plenty of files there!

```
$ cd /bin

$ pwd

$ ls
```

 The **ls** command displays a sorted list of files in the working directory. Because there are so many files in the **/bin** directory, the list will scroll off the screen before you have time to read it. You can suspend scrolling by holding the `CTRL` key and pressing `S`. To quit suspension of scrolling, type `CTRL-Q`.

Instructions	Rules about UNIX filenames

UNIX allows up to 14 characters for a filename. Any combination of characters including numbers can be used except **/**, but the characters < > ? * { } [ ] = should be avoided as they can make file processing both difficult and confusing.
 UNIX filenames are case-sensitive, so the filenames MENU.text and menu.text are quite distinct.
 Filename extensions can be of any length, and program extensions such as .com .exe .bat are not required by the UNIX system. Compilers and applications software have their own conventions, e.g:

.c   C program source file
.h   C include or header file

.old   earlier version program script
.sql   SQL database program script
.lis   list file   }   to be sent to
.rpt   report file   }   the print queue

Activity 7.3	Refining the directory list

To list a single file, type **ls** [*filename*], e.g.

```
$ ls who
```

When a command fails, an error message is usually displayed. If the program file **who** is not located in the working directory, **ls** will display an error message.

The program file **who** is normally found in **/bin**.

To make sure that you see what this particular error message looks like on your system, type

```
$ ls nonsense
```

You can list a directory outside the current working directory without having to move into it:

```
$ cd
```                            — change to your personal working directory

```
$ pwd
```                            — check its pathname

```
$ ls /etc
```                            — list the files in the /etc directory

Activity 7.4   Wild-card characters and brackets

The wild characters ∗ and ? should be familiar to DOS users. They can be used with many UNIX commands.

```
$ ls /etc/a*
```  — lists all files beginning with lower case a

Try other combinations of characters and the asterisk.

The question mark wild-card is used to display files with a variable character in a particular position in the filename, e.g: the command **ls nl????** will list only those files beginning with 'nl' and having only four further characters. For example it will list files such as *nlcode* and *nltemp*, but not *nlpostings*.

Files beginning with a range of characters can be selected for listing by enclosing the range within square brackets.

To list all files beginning with the letters a to f, type

```
$ ls /bin/[a-f]*
```

What output does the following command produce?

```
$ ls /bin/[b,g]*
```

Key words   **pwd**
                     ls
                     cd

Task 8   **Making sense of file listings**

Objectives

To understand the parts of a full file listing.
To display a listing one screen at a time.
To interpret the permission flags.

Instructions

the − l switch and the filter command **more**

You can get a lot more information in the listing by including the − l switch after the command **ls**, i.e.

```
$ ls -1
```

Instead of pressing `CTRL-S` to suspend scrolling of the output from ls − l, you can **pipe** the output from ls − l into another command called **more**.

   more is a type of command called a **filter** and it displays one screen of data and then prints `---more----` at the bottom to tell you that there are more screens to follow. You can then press the `SPACEBAR` to display the next complete screenful, or you can press `ENTER` to display further lines one by one, e.g.

```
$ ls -1 | more
```

The significance of the 'pipeline' symbol will be explained in greater depth in Task 17.

Note: IBM's implementation of UNIX is called AIX and it does not support the filter command **more**. AIX has its own version called **pg**. Therefore, on an AIX system you would type

```
$ ls -1 | pg
```

Activity 8.1

How to interpret the full listing

List the files in the root directory:

```
$ ls -1 /
```

The full ls − l display extends to seven columns, e.g:

1 PERMISSIONS	2 GROUP	3 USER	4 LINKS	5 BYTES	6 DATE & TIME	7 FILENAME
-rwxrwxrw-	1	root		339	Feb 5 15:34	backup.log
drwxrwxrwx	1	unix		512	Sep 24 15:38	bin
drwxrwxrwx	1	oracle		512	Dec 13 12:24	dba
drwxrwxrwx	1	dos		512	Nov 20 12:38	dos
drwxrwxrwx	1	unix		512	Sep 24 15:47	etc
drwxrwxrwx	1	user1		512	Oct 20 04:27	files
-rw--w--w-	1	root	2,	20568	Feb 12 21:09	nlpost.cb.06
-rwxrwxrw-	1	unix		797	Sep 5 1989	profile.ksh
drwxrwxrwx	1	root		512	Dec 13 16:10	qc2
-rwxrwxrw-	1	root		5746	Dec 21 02:34	spinrite.rpt
drw-rw-rw-	10	user1	1,	512	Jan 10 10:24	spool
drwxrwxrwx	1	stats		512	Oct 19 11:01	spss

The first column of the display contains a set of character codes which determine the permitted access rights over the files, e.g:

```
drwxrw-r--
-rw-rw-rw-
```

Except for the very first character, each subsequent character in the permissions field can be set by the owner of the file to determine which users can access that file or directory.

Instructions

The first character code

In UNIX, directories as well as all devices including disk drives and printers are considered to be files. The first character tells you what the entry refers to:

d = a directory
c = a character device, such as a printer or terminal (tty)
b = a block device, such as a disk drive
− = an ordinary file

In the listing on p. 18 there are directories and ordinary files only.

The next nine characters tell you about access permissions. There are three kinds of access: read, write and execute (rwx). There are also three levels of user access, 1: the owner, 2: the group and 3: other users.

The first group of three characters specifies the owner's access, the second three characters specify the group access while the third group of three specifies other users' access.

Read permission allows a user (or user's process) to read the contents of a file or directory.

Write permission allows a user to modify a file, or to create or delete files within a directory.

Execute permission means that a user can execute or 'run' a program file, or search a directory for data and file information.

Columns 2 to 7 of the full listing

2 GROUP: The Group to which the user belongs

3 USER: The id of the owner of the file

4 LINKS: The number of links that the file has to other files and directories

5 BYTES: The extent or length of the file in bytes

6 DATE: The date and time of the most recent update

7 NAME: The name of the file

Activity 8.2   Interpreting the permission characters

The first character indicates that the file is an ordinary file	The next three characters tell you the access for the owner

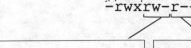

These three characters tell you about group access	The last three characters tell you the access for everyone else

```
-rw-rw-rw-
```
— a file set to read and write for everyone, i.e. all three levels of user

```
crw-rw----
```
— a character device, read and write for owner and group

```
drwx------
```
— a directory, full access for owner only

Now write down what you think the following permissions mean:

```
-r--r-----
```

```
-rw-r--r--
```

```
drw-rw-r--
```

```
brwxrwxrwx
```

Activity 8.3   The full range of switches with **ls**

A number of other switches can be used with **ls**. Certain special files that begin with a dot such as **.profile** are not listed unless you include the **–a** (all) switch. Switches can be combined together. So, to produce a long list of *all* files, type

```
$ ls -al
```

To list all directories below the current path, use the **–R** option; you will certainly need to pipe the output through **more**

```
$ ls -alR ¦ more
```

Now try deliberately using an invalid switch to force the error message that lists the valid switches. See what effect these switches have.

Key words   read
execute
access
permissions
more
pg
filter

Task 9   Subdirectories and pathnames

Objectives

To understand the directory tree structure.
To create your own subdirectories.
To move about the tree structure.

Instructions

You will create your own branch of the directory tree structure below your working directory which for the purpose of this Task we shall call **/user/joe**.

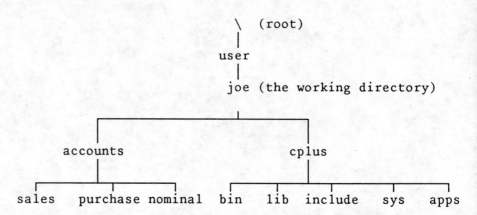

```
              \   (root)
              |
            user
              |
            joe  (the working directory)
```
```
      accounts                        cplus
```
```
sales  purchase  nominal   bin  lib  include  sys  apps
```

The two branches of the tree are to be set up so that an accounts package can be installed in **/user/joe/accounts**. The data files relating to the sales, purchase and nominal ledgers will then be stored in their respective directories at the next level. The other branch of the tree is to be prepared for the installation of a C compiler called CPLUS.

Activity 9.1

Making new directories

First make sure that you are in your home directory

```
$ cd

$ pwd
```

e.g.   `/user/joe`

   The home directory is the **parent directory** of accounts and cplus. To make directories you will use the **mkdir** command:

```
$ mkdir accounts
```

   Check that the directory has been created by listing it:

e.g. `$ ls -l accounts`

PERMISSIONS	LINKS	USER	GROUP	SIZE	DATE	TIME	FILENAME
drwxrwxrwx	2	joe	users	32	Apr 5	14:38	accounts

Now make the directory **cplus** by typing

```
$ mkdir cplus

$ ls -1 cplus
```

Activity 9.2   Creating directories further down the tree

To make a directory you must be in the parent directory. Therefore, to make the directories called sales, purchase and nominal you must first change to the parent directory which is the newly created directory accounts:

```
$ cd accounts

$ pwd

  /user/joe/accounts

$ mkdir sales purchase nominal

$ ls -1
```

   Note that you can make several directories simultaneously by including them as a parameter list after the command **mkdir**

Activity 9.3   Finishing off the **cplus** branch of your tree

To set up the cplus branch of the tree, you must first change to the cplus directory.

You can do this in either of two ways:

1 by including the full path of the cplus directory, e.g:

```
$ cd /user/joe/cplus
```

If you get an error message it is because you have forgotten to substitute *your* working directory path for **/user/joe**

2 by dropping back to the common parent directory,

```
$ cd ..          (cd 'dot dot') – takes you back one level at a time then
                 changing to the required directory.

$ cd cplus
```

These two steps can be combined into one, i.e.

```
$ cd ../cplus
```

Once you are in the cplus directory you should be able to work out how to make the directories at the next level. If you get stuck, the answer is on p. 109

Activity 9.4   Moving around your tree

Change to the new directory below cplus called **bin** by typing:

```
$ cd bin
```

```
$ pwd
```

The path is quite long now, **/user/joe/cplus/bin**

Now try typing **cd   /bin**

```
$ cd /bin
```

```
$ pwd
```

```
  /bin
```

Do not forget that there is another directory called 'bin' which is a 'child' of the root directory.

Change back to your 'bin' directory by including the full path in the cd command:

```
e.g. $ cd /user/joe/cplus/bin
```

Now use the 'cd dot dot' combination to move to the sister directories of /user/joe/ cplus/bin, e.g.:

```
$ cd ../lib
```

```
$ pwd
```

Activity 9.5   Sizing the filestore

If you are likely to create a number of directories and files, you will need to know how much disk space they take up and how much disk space is left. There are two commands for doing this:

du reports on disk use.
If you give no parameter, **du** reports on the number of 512 byte blocks of every directory in the system! It is therefore better to specify a path as the commands parameter, e.g.:

```
$ du /disk0b/tetra

14751   /disk0b/tetra/bin
15055   /disk0b/tetra/sys
9287    /disk0b/tetra/tutor
39340   /disk0b/tetra
```

df reports on the amount of disk space free in 512 byte blocks, e.g.:

```
$ df

/         (/dev/dmcf0a ):   248814 blocks
/disk0b (/dev/dmcf0b ):   184892 blocks
/usr      (/dev/dmcf1a ):   282004 blocks
```

This display came from a small mini-computer with two 315 MByte hard disk drives which are designated dmcf0 and dmcf1 in the device directory /dev.

The first disk has been formatted into two units or **partitions** called **dmcf0a** and **dmcf0b**. The first partition, dmcf0a, has been mounted onto the root directory, and the second partition, dmcf0b, onto a directory rather unimaginatively called /disk0b.

The second disk, **dmcf1a**, has been formatted as a single partition and has been mounted quite transparently onto the UNIX filestore as the directory **/usr**.

Troubleshooting   If you have difficulty making any of the directories in the Activities above, it could be because you are not in the correct 'parent' directory.

You should not be able to create new directories at a level higher than your home directory. If, inadvertently you attempt to make a directory with the root directory as the parent, the error message **Access denied** should appear. This is because you should not have write access permission over the root directory.

Key words	
	pwd
	mkdir
	bin

Task 10   # Searching the tree for files

Objectives   To find a file in the directory tree.

Instructions   Most UNIX filestores are large in comparison with those on Personal Computers. The directory structures that proliferate over hundreds or even thousands of megabytes of disk space can make it time consuming and frustrating to find files. The best thing to do is to keep a note of the directory where files have been put.

Documentation is often the task that is least well carried out, even by computer professionals who ought to know better. UNIX provides a command called **find** that scans through the directory structure starting from any point that you specify for a filename or part of a filename.

Activity 10.1   How to find a file whose name you know

Most UNIX systems will have a file called **passwd** that contains data about users and their ids. To discover where the file is located, type the command **find** exactly as it is shown below:

```
$ find  /  -name passwd -print
```

e.g.   `/bin/passwd`
         `/etc/passwd`

The output from the command tells you that there are two files called **passwd**, one in the **/bin** directory, the other in the **/etc** directory.

The command syntax

The syntax of the command **find** is a bit more complicated than that of commands you have met before. There are four parameters to the command each separated by white space:

```
            1      2       3        4

$ find  /  -name  passwd  -print
```

1 The first parameter tells **find** where to start looking for the file(s).
   / means begin at the root directory.
   . means start at the working directory and carry on down that branch of the tree

2 There are several options that can be used in parameter 2. The most common are the **–name** option which tells **find** that the data in parameter 3 refers to a file or directory name, and **–user** which looks for all files owned by a certain user.

3 This is the name of the file(s) or user's files you are trying to locate.

4 The option **–print** causes the output to be 'printed' on the screen.
   When UNIX describes data as being 'printed', in fact it is displayed on a VDU screen. This because, in the beginning, terminals were 'teletype' printer terminals rather than VDUs.

To practice locating various files starting at the root, substitute the following filenames into position 3 of the command: grep   head   tty0

Activity 10.2   Locating files starting further down the tree

If you know that a file is located somewhere below your working directory it will be quicker to start from there, rather than having to scan the whole tree from the root up.

For the purpose of this Task you will need to create a dummy file in the directory **accounts** that you made in the previous task.

```
$ cd

$ pwd

$ cd accounts

$ echo dummy >test
```
The last command echoes the word 'dummy' into a file called 'test'.
Now drop back a level in the directory structure:

```
$ cd ..
```
and use **find** to locate the test file

```
$ find . -name test -print
```
You will find it useful to see how much longer it takes to find the file starting from the root. Also, there is a possibility that there may be other files called 'test' lurking around the system.

Activity 10.3   Looking for files belonging to a certain user

Try substituting for 'fred' below a user id that you know belongs to your system:

```
$ find . -user fred -print
```
If you cannot think of anyone's id, try using the **who** command.

Warning: **find** cannot search directories to which you have no right of access. In this case you will get an error message such as:

cannot chdir to /fitchett

Key words	find	-print
	-name	-user

Task 11   Identifying types of files

Objective

To be able to distinguish between the various types of ordinary file.

Instructions

In the UNIX file-system there are four main categories of file:
- character device files e.g. terminals, printers
- block device files e.g. disk drives
- directories
- ordinary files

As you have already seen in Task 8, the command **ls –l** gives a long listing whose first field tells you what the main category is (*see* p. 19).

There are various different types of ordinary files and ls –l cannot discriminate between them.

File type	*Examples*
1 English language text files	reports, printer spool files, documents
2 Program source files	uncompiled C programs
3 UNIX shell scripts	programs constructed from UNIX commands like MS–DOS batch files
4 Binary data files	database files, system data
5 Executable program files	compiled files consisting mainly of binary instructions to the CPU

Examples 1 to 3 are all stored in human readable ASCII format. They can normally be accessed quite easily and their contents displayed on a terminal or printer.

Examples 4 and 5 are in binary or 'machine' code form and cannot be displayed directly.

Activity 11.1

Using the command 'file' to identify different types of file

To investigate the file **who**, use **find** to discover which directory it belongs to, e.g.

```
$ find / -name who -print
/bin/who
```
(In some UNIX versions **who** is located in the directory **/usr/bin**.)

The command **file** will report on a single file if you pass the exact filename or path to the command as a parameter, e.g.

```
    $ file /bin/who
```
                                                  (*or* file /user/bin/who)
```
e.g. /bin/who: pure executable
```

This tells you that **who** is a binary code program file.

The usual wild-card characters * and ? can be used with **file**. So, to get a list of files in the parent directory of your home directory, type:

```
$ cd                 – change directory to home directory

$ file  ../*  – report on all files in the parent
                          directory
```

You can pass a list of files to **file**
```
$ file  /bin/ls  /usr/lib/menu  accounts
```

Do not forget that every UNIX file system is different, so it is impossible to make concrete suggestions as to the parameters you can try passing to a command. You will need to experiment and substitute different filenames and paths for the ones in the example on p. 28.

Move around the directory tree and use a combination of ls, find and file to identify at least one example of the five file types described above. The following Activity explains how to do this.

Activity 11.2

Exploring the passwd files

There are *two* passwd files. One is a text file with details of user ids, passwords and associated information. The second is the executable program file which runs when you type the command **passwd**.

Find out what these two files are and where they can be found.

To locate a file, use the **find** command.
```
$ find / –name pass*  –print
```

Once you know where the two files live, change (cd) to the appropriate directories and do the following checks:

Use **ls –l** to see which permission flags have been set.

Use the **file** command on each version of the passwd file.

What can you deduce about the two files? Write down your findings before turning to the answers on p. 109.

Key words	**text files**
	source files
	shell scripts
	binary instructions
	executable code

Task 12   **Displaying the contents of a file**

Objective   To display or print the contents of an ASCII file.
                      To display embedded text in a binary file.

Instructions   So far you have been looking at the information displayed about files by using the
                      commands **ls** and **file**. You will now see what is inside the file.

Activity 12.1   Displaying a file with the commands **cat** and **more**

                      The name cat is derived from the word 'concatenate' meaning to link (as in a chain).

                      First of all you will need to locate a suitable file to display. You have already done
                      this in previous Tasks.
                          Move to a directory where there is a file which you know consists of English
                      language text or ASCII characters, then use the filter command **cat** to copy the file
                      from the file store to your console.

                      ```
                      $ cd /etc
                      ```

                      ```
                      $ file passwd        (this will double-check that it is an ASCII file)
                      ```

                      ```
                      $ cat passwd
                      ```

                      If the file is longer than 24 lines, the display will scroll up the screen and the top of
                      the file will vanish. Remember that you can suspend scrolling by holding down
                      the CTRL key and pressing S. Pressing CTRL-Q will reactivate the display.
                          If the file to be displayed is long, you can use **more** to display it one screen at a
                      time:

                      ```
                      $ more passwd
                      ```

                      Alternatively, you could pipe the output of cat through **more**

                      ```
                      $ cat passwd ¦ more
                      ```

Troubleshooting   If you have a problem with *more*, it may be because your version of UNIX supports the
                      alternative command **pg**. If you suspect this to be the case, substitute the command **pg**
                      for all occurrences of **more** in the text.

Activity 12.2 Investigating files in other directories

cat is the prototypical UNIX filter. It takes its input from a file or device and outputs the unaltered data to the terminal unless directed otherwise.

The general form of the command is

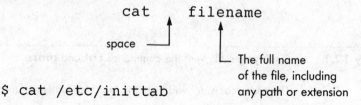

space ⤴ ⤴ The full name
of the file, including
any path or extension

e.g. `$ cat /etc/inittab`

Note: Only text files or data files in standard ASCII character format can be displayed using **cat**. If you try to read a program file which consists of binary machine code instructions, the screen will be filled with garbage, the terminal may beep at you and will probably 'hang up' on you as well!

Unlike DOS command files which have the extension .com or .exe, UNIX program files can have any kind of name. The only way to know for certain whether it is safe to display a file is to test it out using the **file** command first.

Now change to another directory and look for suitable files to display. If the command does not work it is probably because you do not have read permission over that file or directory. You will need to use a combination of the commands **cd**, **ls**, **file** and **cat**.

Activity 12.3 Looking into binary files

There is a command called **strings** which displays any strings of embedded text that may exist inside an otherwise unreadable binary file. It is quite instructive to use **strings** on some of the commands you have met so far. Most of these commands live in directory **/bin**.

`$ cd /bin`

`$ strings ls ¦more`

Try investigating files with the powerful combination of **find**, **ls**, **file**, **cat** and **strings**.

Key words	file
	cat
	concatenate
	embedded text
	strings

Section C: File housekeeping utilities ━━━

In this section you will copy, move and rename files within the tree structure. It is important to learn how to delete unwanted files and directories safely. You will also learn how to protect files and directories from the unwelcome attentions of other users.

Task 13	**Copying files within the directory tree**

Objective

To learn how to use the **cp** command.

Instructions

You will copy some files into your working directory and into the new directory **accounts** that you made in Task 9. The general form of the **cp** command is:

```
cp  sourcefile(s)  targetfile
```

There are four basic points to remember:

1 **cp** makes a new copy of the file leaving the existing *sourcefile* unchanged.

2 The new copy will overwrite a file of the same name in the *targetfile* directory.

3 If there is more than one *sourcefile* then *targetfile* must be a directory.

4 You must have permission to **read** the *sourcefile* and to **write** to the *targetfile*.

Study these examples (but do not try them – you would need access to these files):

```
1 cp  myfile  myfile.old
```

This example makes a copy of **myfile** and calls it **myfile.old**. Both files are in the current working directory.

It is a good idea to use **cp** to make a new version of a file before editing the original so that if anything were to go wrong you would still have the earlier version of the file with the suffix **.old**

```
2 cp  /usr/joe/project5  .
```

Here cp copies the file **project5** from the directory /usr/joe to the working directory without changing its name. Notice that a complete pathname can be incorporated in the *sourcefile* parameter. In this example the *targetfile* parameter consists of the single dot which stands for the working directory.

```
3 cp  temp.msg  /dev/tty5
```

The file temp.msg in the working directory is copied to the character device **tty5**, located in the directory /dev. Remember that UNIX treats devices as files, so the data will be copied to that device provided that it is **online**, i.e. that it is powered up and connected to the CPU. Typically, **tty5** would refer to a terminal or a printer.

You must be careful when copying data directly to a character device. If the device is disconnected the command will fail harmlessly. If you try to copy a binary file to a terminal or printer it could cause it to 'hang'. You should therefore use the command **file** as you did in the examples in Task 11.

If someone else is running applications software and you copy a file to their terminal, it could wipe off their work. To prevent this from happening to you, find out whether the command **mesg n** (*see* Task 3) will stop someone from hi-jacking your terminal by copying their work to it.

If /dev/tty5 is a printer, a collision could occur if another user simultaneously tried to copy a file directly to it by this method. Such problems are sorted out by the printer scheduler which allocates print jobs to a queue and deals with them in an orderly fashion. See Task 19.

4 cp client.data /dd2/oracle/dbs

You may wonder how UNIX copies files from one disk drive to another when there are no drive letters such as **A**: and **C**: as there are in DOS. In example 4, the file in the working directory is copied to another disk drive which has been **mounted** on to the tree structure as a directory called **dd2**. This is an entirely arbitrary **logical name** for the example system's second disk drive.

Removeable media such as tape cartridges and floppy drives which are not mounted on to the file tree have data copied to and from them by other commands such as **cpio**.

Activity 13.1	Copying a single file to the working directory
	Copy the file **inittab** from /etc to the working directory which should also be your home directory:
	`$ cd`
	`$ cp /etc/inittab .` Remember to type the dot!
	`$ ls -l`

Activity 13.2	Copying a group of files using 'wild' characters
	`$ cp /bin/e* .`
	`$ ls -l`
	`$ cp /dev/tty? .`
	`$ ls -l`
	Note that UNIX does not echo the name(s) of the file(s) while it copies them. That is why you need to check that the files have actually been copied by using the **ls** command.

Activity 13.3	Copying files to a different target directory or filename

Copy the message of the day (motd) to your working directory, calling the new copy **motd.old**

```
$ cp /etc/motd  ./motd.old

$ ls -l
```

Copy all the files in the /bin directory that begin with the letters g or k to the new directory **accounts**

```
$ cp /bin/[g,k]* ./accounts

$ ls -l accounts
```

You can specify a list of files to be copied as a series of parameters. The last parameter is always the target directory. In the following example the first two parameters refer to files to be copied and the third parameter, the dot, refers to the working directory.

```
$ cp /etc/inittab  /etc/passwd .
```

The files initials and **passwd** should have been copied from the directory **/etc** to your working directory.

Troubleshooting If the *sourcefile* parameter specifies a number of files and the *targetfile* parameter is not a directory, you will get an error message telling you that the target file must be a directory.

One of the biggest problems in UNIX is knowing where you are, i.e. what your working directory is, and also knowing where the sourcefiles are located. If any of the above examples did not work, it could be because:

- the path to the sourcefiles is different for your system
- the target directory accounts does not exist
- the working directory was not the parent of accounts, therefore the relative path **./accounts** is invalid
- the source or target files (or directories) do not permit read or write access. You should be able to check this by using the **ls –l** command to see how the permission flags are set. See Task 8, p 18.

Key words	logical name
	sourcefile
	targetfile
	online

Task 14   **Moving and renaming files**

Objectives

To create simple practice files using **touch**.
To consolidate some previously used commands.
To move and rename the practice files using the **mv** command.

Instructions

Unlike **cp** which creates a new copy of a file leaving the sourcefile intact, **mv** does not retain the original sourcefile.
   The form of the command will be familiar to you:

mv   *sourcefile(s)*   *targetfile*

sourcefile(s) can be:

a single file	example 1: mv	`mv myfile.old myfile`
a group of files	example 2: mv	`mv *.old ./oldfiles`
a list of files	example 3: mv	`mv file1 file2 ./accounts`
a whole directory	example 4: mv	`mv ./dbs ./database`

If *sourcefiles* is a group or list of files, then *targetfile* must be a directory. Conversely, *targetfile* can only be a single file if *sourcefile* is a single file.
   Write down what you expect to happen in the examples above. Compare your notes with the answers on p. 109. Do not attempt to try out the commands yet.

Warning: Like **cp**, **mv** overwrites an existing targetfile with the same name. Because the sourcefile is not retained, you can end up losing files if you are careless. What could go wrong in the following example?

example 5   `mv memo3.joe backup`

followed sometime later by:

`mv fault.log backup`

Activity 14.1   Creating practice files

Because of the inherent danger with **mv**, you need to make some practice files, which you can do using the **touch** command.
   First make sure that your home directory is the working directory:

`$ cd`

Then type:

`$ touch myfile.old`

36

After typing the command above, there will be a new file called **myfile.old** which you can examine.

```
$ ls -l myfile.old
```

```
$ file myfile.old
```

Touch creates an empty file if one of that name does not exist in the working directory. Using the same technique, make another new file called **letter3.old**.

```
$ touch letter3.old
```

You should now be able to make some dummy files. They will need to have the names listed below. The general form of the command is:

```
touch file1 [file2 etc...]
```

The files you need to make are:

```
ibmterm.old
list.old
n1.data
s1.data
p1.data
```

You will also need to make new directories called **dbs** and **oldfiles**, as explained on p. 22.

Activity 14.2   Moving the practice files

Begin by following example 1 above:

```
$ ls -l my*
```

```
$ mv myfile.old myfile
```

```
$ ls -l my*
```

Now try example 2:

```
$ ls -l *.old
```

```
$ mv *.old  ./oldfiles
```

```
$ ls -l *.old
```

```
$ ls -l oldfiles
```

You should be able to move the files **n1data** and **s1data** to **/accounts** by following the format of example 3 above.

| Activity 14.3 | Moving a directory |

First copy some files into the new directory **dbs**

```
$ cp * ./dbs

$ ls -l dbs

$ mv ./dbs ./database

$ ls -l dbs

$ ls -l database
```

See what happens to the contents of the renamed directory database if you type the command:

```
$ mv ./accounts ./database
```

e.g.   `mv: database exists`

mv prevents you from inadvertently moving a directory to one that already exists, but it does overwrite single files of the same name.

Key words	echo
	mv
	touch

Task 15   **Removing files and directories**

Objective   To remove unwanted files and directories safely and selectively.

Instructions   Removing or deleting unwanted files is an important task because disk storage is finite. Old or seldomly accessed files need to be purged from time to time especially on a system where there are many users.
Files are removed by the **rm** command:

```
rm -[switch] file1 [file2 etc...]
```

e.g. `rm -i nl001.lis nl002.rpt`

There are three optional switches:

- –i   interactive; before the file is removed the user is asked to confirm this action by typing **y**

- –f   erases write protected files belonging to the owner only

- –r   recursively erases directories *and their contents* without warning. Formidably dangerous!

Activity 15.1   Removing files from your working directory

You must be in your home directory before starting this activity.

```
$ cd;pwd
```
– two commands may be entered separated by a semicolon

```
$ ls -l
```
– list files and select unwanted ones

In Task 13 you copied the files **inittab** and **motd** to your working directory. Now is the time to remove them.

```
$ rm inittab
```

```
$ ls inittab
```

You can remove more than one file at once by including a parameter list:

```
$ ls -l
```

e.g. `$ rm -i motd  motd.old myfile.old`

You must choose your own files to remove.
You can remove a group of files by using the wild characters in the usual way.

```
e.g.  $ rm *.data
```

Activity 15.2   Removing directories

The safe command to remove directories is **rmdir**.

```
rmdir directory1 [directory2 etc ...]
```

However, the following rules apply
- you must be the owner of the directory.
- you must be in the parent directory, i.e. the level above the target directory.
- the target directory must be empty of files.

Try to remove your accounts directory:

```
$ cd;pwd

$ rmdir accounts
```

e.g. `rmdir: accounts not empty`

If the directory contains files, **rmdir** will protect against inadvertent erasure.

Activity 15.3   Using rm to remove directories

As a UNIX directory is a file itself, and since **rm** removes files, it should also remove directories. **rm** will only do this when the **–r** switch is invoked.

In Task 14 you made the directory **oldfiles**. Try removing it using **rmdir**. The command should not succeed because the directory **oldfiles** contains files. You could make **oldfiles** the working directory and then list and remove the files if they are no longer required.

However, as you know that **oldfiles** is full of unwanted material, you can delete the files and the directory in one operation by typing:

```
$ cd;pwd                          (this double-checks your whereabouts)

$ rm -r oldfiles

ls -l oldfiles                    (the directory has now gone)
```

There are times when you want to clear out a whole branch of a directory tree, and **rm –r** speeds up the process greatly. As you can see, the command needs to be treated with the utmost care.

If you want to be more cautious you can combine the **–i** and **–r** switches together:

```
$ rm -ir database
```

Troubleshooting   These are common error messages that you may see with both commands:

cannot remove	no permission on source
non-existent	file or directory is not in working directory
directory not empty	you cannot remove a directory with files in it
cannot read	no permission on target file or directory
illegal option	you have tried to use an invalid switch
permission denied	you do not have permission to use the command

Key words	rm
	rmdir

Task 16   Ownership and access to files

Objectives

To control other users' access to your files.

Instructions

The rwx characters which are displayed when you list files using the command **ls –l**
control the access to files by the owner, the group and other users. They are described
fully in Task 8 on p. 18. They can be set by the owner of the file or by the system
administrator. The function and purpose of the file together with the legitimate use that
the user community as a whole needs to make of it are the factors that should govern
the precise settings of the file permissions.

Activity 16.1

Looking at the default settings

Make up a practice file called **homefiles** by following these instructions:

```
$ cd;pwd
```

```
$ cat > homefiles (Return ↵)
echo "Files in the HOME directory\n" (Return ↵)
cd;pwd (Return ↵)
ls -l ¦ more (Return ↵)
(Ctrl)+(d)
```

(substitute **pg** if your system does not have **more**)

Look at the way the permission flags have been set for this new file:

```
$ ls -l
```

```
e.g. -rw-rw-rw-  1  joe  users 55 Nov 19 10:23  homefiles
```

The file that you have just made is a collection of UNIX shell commands, similar to a
DOS batch file. It should therefore be possible to execute the command simply by
typing its name:

```
$ homefiles
```

If the command fails, look again at the permissions for the file. The usual default is
-rw-rw-rw indicating that everyone has read and write access to the file, but nobody
has execute permission, so not even the owner can run the program.

Activity 16.2	Changing the permissions

You will use the command **chmod** to change the mode of access which will enable your new command homefiles to run.

```
$ chmod +x homefiles   (adds execute permission for everyone)

$ ls -l
```

e.g. `-rwxrwxrwx`   etc

Now you can run the program by typing its name:

```
$ homefiles
```

Explanation

If **homefiles** executes correctly, it should first echo the heading:

```
Files in the HOME directory
```

followed by a new line. (The **escape** character ▮ at the end of the echo line tells the shell to interpret the character **n** as a signal to print a new line.)

The next two lines of the program print the home directory path, before giving a full directory listing which is piped through **more** (or **pg**).

UNIX programs made up of shell commands are called **shell scripts**. Many useful utility programs that make life easier for users are created by users themselves from the powerful raw materials of UNIX commands.

Suppose you have created a utility that you want everyone to be able to use, but which you do not want others to mess about with or delete. A sensible set of permissions would be:

```
-rwxr-xr-x
```

What does this combination signify? (Answer on p. 110.)

You can change the flags from **-rwxrwxrwx** to **-rwxr-xr-x** by typing:

```
$ chmod go=rx      (Group & Other = Read/eXecute)

$ ls -l
```

If you want the group to have read/execute permission and others to have execute permission only, you could type:

chmod uses the following mnemonic codes:

u	User	+	Add permission	r	Read permission
g	Group	–	Remove permission	w	Write permission
o	Other	=	Enable setting	x	Execute permission

Activity 16.3   Changing permissions by numeric codes

Some people find it easier to change permissions by using a set of number codes:

r=4   w=2   x=1

The codes are added up for each group of three characters.

```
1  rw-rw-rw-
   42 42 42
 = 6  6  6    so chmod 666 sets the pattern: rw-rw-rw-

2  rwx-rx--x
   421 21  1
 = 7   3  1   chmod 731 gives rwx-rw--x
```

Use **touch** to set up four practice files called permit1 to permit4. Experiment with various combinations of permissions to see the effect. It would be a good idea to test the effectiveness of these experiments with another user on a neighbouring terminal.

```
$ cd;pwd
```

```
$ touch permit1 permit2 etc
```

```
$ ls -l permit?
```

Now do the following experiments:

```
$ chmod 777 permit1
```

```
$ chmod 555 permit2
```

Look at the way the characters are set now:

```
$ ls -l permit?
```

Set permit3 to read only, i.e: r--r--r--

```
$ chmod 444 permit3
```

Now try and remove the file:

```
$ rm permit3
```

Set permit4 to write only:

```
$ chmod 222 permit4
```

Try to copy it:

```
$ cp permit4 permit5
```

In order to copy a file, you need **read** permission on the source file and **write** permission on the target.

Activity 16.4   Protecting directories

You can also protect directories. To do this, try to team up with another user to see the effect of trying to access another user's directories.

```
$ cd;pwd

$ mkdir secure              (make a directory called secure)

$ cp * ./secure             (copy some files to it)

$ ls -l secure              (check out the default permissions)
```

Change to each other's ./secure directories, list files, change a filename with **mv**, and generally wreak havoc. When you have finished having fun, change back to your own directory and list it (assuming that there are some files left intact!).

To prevent this sort of action you can shut other users out altogether.

```
$ chmod 770 secure

$ ls -l secure
```

e.g. `drwxrwx---  etc`

Now try to change into each other's directories.
Don't forget that you may need to keep other members of your group out:

```
$ chmod 700 secure

$ ls -l secure
```

e.g. `drwx------`

Sometimes it is useful to be able to list files in someone else's directory. You could grant **read** permission only to that directory:

```
$ chmod 744 secure

$ ls -l secure

drwx--r--r--
```

e.g. `$ ls -l ../joe/secure`   (list joe's secure directory)

Finally, you can try updating each other's files by echoing a phrase and redirecting it into one of their permit files, e.g.

```
$ echo Kilroy was here >> ../joe/permit1
```

This example assumes that there is another user called **joe** whose home directory is on the same level as yours.

joe and you should be working out various ways of keeping each other at a safe distance, by allowing access to some files and directories but not others.

Activity 16.5   Linking files to other directories

Controlling access does not have to be a negative activity: the whole point of a UNIX system is that it is a community of users. A multi-user system should enable users to work together by sharing data and communicating information where possible. Where more than one user needs access to a file it could be placed in a directory which is commonly accessible. Alternatively, the single file can be linked to a number of directories. Consider this example which assumes that user **joe** owns a file called **phone.list**:

```
$ cd;pwd
/user/joe

$ cp phone.list  ../sue
```

After entering the commands above, the original copy of the file **phone.list** will remain in the directory **/user/joe** and there will be a second copy of the file in the directory **/user/sue**.

If you now update the file by typing:

```
$ echo "Susan Lee   407   334   Marketing">>phone.list
```

a new record will be appended to the copy of the file in the working directory but not in your colleague's directory. What you could have done was to **link** the file to the other directory rather than copy it there:

```
$ rm ../sue/phone.list

$ ln phone.list ../sue/phone.list

$ ls -l ../sue/ph*
```

e.g. `-rw-rw-rw-  1 joe  users 5  Nov 19 10:23  phone.list`

It will appear as if the file has two separate existences in each of the two directories. However, if you try updating the file from either directory, the change will be apparent in the other.

Key words   chmod
shell script
ln

Task 17   **Making simple text files**

Objectives   To redirect output from **echo** and **cat** into a file.
To send files into the **electronic mail** system.

Instructions   **echo** takes input from the keyboard as part of the command line and sends it directly to the terminal unless otherwise directed.

Activity 17.1   Simple redirection to a file

```
$ echo Here is an announcement

Here is an announcement
```

The output can be redirected into a file by means of the **redirection** signs `>` and `>>`

```
$ cd;pwd

$ echo "Name          Room   Extension" >phone.list

$ cat phone.list

Name          Room   Extension
```

The string of characters **Name   Room Extension** is redirected into a new file which is opened for the purpose. If a file called **phones.list** already exists it will be overwritten, unless it has been protected.

The string was put inside quotation marks to preserve the amount of white space between the first two words.

```
$ echo Michael Turnbull  302   405 >>phone.list

$ cat phone.list

Name          Room  Extension
Michael Turnbull 302    405
```

Redirecting with two greater than signs `>` `>` causes output to be appended to an existing file with the same name.

Activity 17.2 Coping with metacharacters

Metacharacters are characters that have a special meaning to the UNIX shell. The dollar sign is used to indicate variable names. Try this:

```
$ echo HOME
HOME

$ echo $HOME
```

e.g.   `/users/joe`

$HOME is a *shell variable* that contains the absolute path of your home directory. The dollar sign tells UNIX not to echo the word HOME literally, but to display the contents of the variable.

   If you want to echo a sum of money in dollars, typing **echo $4000** will not work. You have to enclose the metacharacter in back-slashes:

```
$ echo \$\4000
```

e.g.   `$4000`

As ▮ is also a metacharacter, it must be wrapped up in itself if it is to be included in a string:

```
$ echo 3\\\4
```

e.g.   `3\4`

Now investigate the following:

```
$ echo "Check this"

$ echo "Check this\n"

$ echo "Check this\e"

$ echo "Part number 345\n\23a"

$ echo "Part number 234\\\23a"
```

Activity 17.3   Using **cat** to add more lines to the file.

echo is a good way to add a single line to a file, but you can use **cat** if there are several lines to add. The principle is similar to the DOS command **copy con**. However, remember that you are not in a word-processor, so you cannot edit out mistakes other than by the backspace ⬅ or DEL key.

```
$ cat >>phone.list
Deborah Adams       308    322  [Return ↵]
David Scott         400    325  [Return ↵]
[Ctrl]+[d]
```

To end the stream of input and close the file press CTRL-D. Use **cat** without the redirection symbols to display the file you have updated:

```
$ cat phone.list
Name                Room   Extension
Michael Turnbull    302    405
Deborah Adams       308    322
David Scott         400    325
```

Activity 17.4   Making and sending a temporary message file

One of the problems you found with the direct mail command **write** was that you had to transmit each line in turn. This can be a problem for the recipient, particularly if you are a slow typist.

   Now that you can make a small file, you can transmit a multi-line message in one action:

```
$ cat > message
Urgent message to all car users!!!! [Return ↵]
[Return ↵]
The car park will be closed this afternoon [Return ↵]
for repairs to the asphalt surface. [Return ↵]
[Return ↵]
Please move your car out by 1230 [Return ↵]
[Return ↵]
P. Snerd,  Clerk of the Works [Return ↵]
[Ctrl]+[d]
```

The message will be stored in the file of the same name. You can check it by using **cat** again:

```
$ cat message
```

Instead of sending the output by default to the terminal, you can **pipe** it to the command **write**. First check that there is a suitable recipient who is logged on:

```
        $ who
e.g.  joe   tty7     15 Mar 12.30
```

```
        $ cat message ¦ write joe
```

Connecting the output of one command to the input of another is done using the pipe symbol ▮ as opposed to connecting the output of a command to a file which uses the redirection symbols ◀ and ▶.

```
e.g.  file1 < command1   ¦ command2 > file2
```

Here command1 reads input from file1 and then produces output which is connected to the input of command2. The output of command2 is sent to file2.

Key words	metacharacter
	pipe
	redirection
	absolute path

Task 18

Basic editing techniques

Objective
To edit and create text files using the editor.

Instructions
So far you have made files using **cat** and **echo. echo** can update a file by appending a single line to the end. If more extensive changes are required, or lines need to be added to the middle of a file, a text editor is necessary.

Various editors can be found on UNIX systems, but the most common and easiest to use is **vi** which is short for 'visual editor'.

Activity 18.1

Adding text to the end of a line

To edit a file type the command **vi *filename***

```
$ vi phone.list
```

The first page of text will be displayed. Any unused lines are depicted by the **tilde** sign ~ . Do not try to type anything at this stage because **vi** is in command mode.

You can move around the file using the cursor arrow keys — assuming that your terminal is capable of this! `CTRL-D` scrolls **D**own 10 lines and `CTRL-U` scrolls **U**p.

To enter text you need to put **vi** into **append** or **insert** mode. Move the cursor to the final character of the first line of the file, (it should be over the n of Extension):

vi is in command mode, so press **a** for append. You can now type two spaces followed by the word **Department**. The first line of the file should now read:

```
Name                    Room    Extension   Department
```

To get out of **append** mode, press the `ESC` (Escape) key. Move the cursor to the end of the next line, and press **a** to append 'Purchasing' to the Department column of Michael Turnbull's entry. Press `ESC` immediately after you have typed in the additional word.

Deborah Adams and David Scott are both in Personnel, so add this department's name to their records. You could make up a new record for another employee and append it to the end of the file.

Do not worry if you find you have added blank lines or cursor control sequences by mistake. You can tidy up later.

Activity 18.2

Inserting text

To insert a new line in the middle of a file, place the cursor at the end of the previous line, press **a** for append, press `ENTER` and type in the line. Do not forget to press `ESC` to escape from append mode before attempting to use the arrow keys.

Add the line

```
Stephen Wilkinson        219    125    Security
```

To insert text in the middle of a line use the command **i** for insert:

Escape to the command line by pressing `ESC` and move the cursor over the **S** of Scott. Press **i** and type the name **Lee**.

Activity 18.3   Tidying up

Having inserted the name Lee between David and Scott, the rest of the record will be mis-aligned. Place the cursor after the name Scott and press **x** to delete some spaces until the numbers line up correctly. Use **a** or **i** to add some more text to the file. If your editing proves to be too ruthless, press `U` to undo the last change that you made. Remember, these mnemonics work only in the context of **vi**.

You can delete an unwanted word by positioning the cursor on the first letter of the word and pressing **dw**, or delete a whole line by pressing **dd**.

Activity 18.4   Saving your work

Everything you type is stored in a temporary memory buffer. To commit your changes permanently to the file press `ESC` to get out of insert or append mode and type **:x** (exit and save).

There are many more commands within **vi**, but the following ones will allow you to do most things:

a	append
i	insert
x	delete one character
dw	delete a word
dd	delete a whole line
u	undo the last edit
.	repeat the last edit
j	join two lines
:w	write to the file and continue editing
:x	exit and save
:	quit without committing any changes

Activity 18.5   Searching for a pattern

Load a text file by typing **vi** followed by the filename, e.g.

```
$ vi phone.list
```

To search for the pattern 'bull', type: /bull

vi searches the file *below* the cursor's current location. If you press SHIFT / followed by the string, **vi** will search the buffer *above* the current cursor position, e.g. **?Name**.

Having located a pattern using / or ? press **n** to find the next occurrence of the pattern down the file, or **N** for the next occurrence up the file.

You can exit by typing **:q**, or **:q!** The **!** mark suppresses warnings from **vi** that the buffer has not been saved.

Activity 18.6   Finishing off the file phone.list

You will need **phone.list** in Section D of the Guide when you will use it to illustrate some file and data processing techniques. Before doing this final edit of the file make another copy of the file and call it **phone.old**.

```
$ vi phone.list
```

Now load phone.list into the editing buffer:

```
$ cp phone.list phone.old
```

You need to edit the file so that each field is separated by a colon. If you use tabs or spaces as delimiters you will run into problems with names like David Lee Scott, which takes up three columns.

The table should look like this when you have finished:

```
Michael Turnbull:302:405:Purchasing
Stephen Wilkinson:219:125:Security
Deborah Adams:308:322:Personnel
David Lee Scott:400:325:Personnel
```

The important point is that the fields are separated by colons; it does not matter what the names and numbers are. Obviously the file will be more meaningful if you add some more records of your own.

The file does not look as good without the spaces, but you can apply various formatting techniques to it later on.

Activity 18.7   Creating a file for the calendar function

The command **calendar** reads a file that you create also called **calendar** in your home directory. It sends any line containing today's or tomorrow's date to standard output.

The dates must be in these formats:

> Jan. 6 or 1/6   i.e. American date month/year

> September 12   *or*   9/12

> */1   the first day of every month

Create a calendar file using **vi:** Choose today's dates and a few days hence. Appointments do not have to be entered in chronological order.

```
$ vi calendar
```

e.g.
```
*/2 Last month's sales report deadline
July 10  9.30 Meeting with Gill Bannatine from Denco
July 10  3.00 Presentation to Board
July 11 10.00 Marketing meeting
July 11 Don't forget Tim's birthday present
July 8  Conference on Global Cooling
```

To test your diary, simply type the command **calendar**.

To ensure that your diary is displayed when you log in, add the command to your **.profile** which is a program that runs first whenever you login.

```
$ echo "calendar\n">>.profile
```

Key words	vi
	visual editor
	append mode
	insert mode
	command mode
	field delimiter
	calendar
	. profile

Task 19   Printing files

Objective   To output data from a file to a printer.

Instructions   There are various ways of outputting data to a printer in a UNIX system. We shall look at two simple methods.

Activity 19.1   Copying data directly to a printer

If you know the terminal number of a printer, you can copy data to it using the **cat** or **cp** (copy) command. This was discussed briefly in Task 13 p. 33). For example, if there was a printer connected to terminal port 8, you could redirect the output of **cat** to that terminal:

```
$ cat phone.list >/dev/tty8
```

Note that UNIX regards the printer as just another file. The **tty** device files are in the directory **/dev**.

It is a good idea to use the command **file** to check that the file you propose to print is a text or ASCII file, otherwise you could cause the printer to 'hang up'. Do not attempt to print executable or binary files.

```
$ file /etc/inittab

$ more /etc/inittab

$ cp /etc/inittab /dev/tty8
```

It is also useful to inspect the file first using **cat** or **more**. When you are certain that the file is readable and that it is really what you want, then copy it to the printer.

You may find that a serial printer has been connected directly to the serial printer port on the CPU. In this case the printer is addressed as **/dev/ptrs**, e.g.

```
$ cat phone.list >/dev/ptrs
```

This method of printing files is fine if the printer is within very easy reach of your terminal. You can then see if the printer is switched on, has paper and is idle. If you have access to a remote printer then it should be managed by the administrator via a scheduling program that queues print jobs in an orderly manner so that collisions do not occur when more than one user requests a printout simultaneously. Print jobs are stored as temporary files called **spool files**. The scheduler removes them as soon as they have been printed.

Investigating the scheduler

You can use the command **lpstat** to give you a report on the current status of the printer:

```
$ lpstat -t
```

e.g.
```
scheduler is running
system default destination: gen
device for gen: /dev/ptrs
device for gen1: /dev/tty08
device for accounts: /dev/tty24

printer gen accepting requests since Feb 12 15:47
gen1 accepting requests since Mar 2 10:41
accounts accepting requests since May 24 11:03
printer accounts disabled since Dec 10 10:32
   -disabled by scheduler: can't open /dev/tty24

printer gen is busy: enabled since Oct 31 12:24
printer gen1 is idle: enabled since Nov 5 10:26

accounts-456    marion   24899 Dec 11 09:21
gen-4739        joe      20843 Dec 12 12:41
gen-4740        root      4256 Dec 12 12:43
etc.
```

Instructions

Interpreting the listing from **lpstat**

Three printers have been installed on the example system: the default printer, **gen** (general printer) which is attached directly to the serial printer port of the CPU; a printer referred to as **gen1** connected to the i/o port tty08; and one called **accounts**, supposedly connected to port tty24. It has been disabled because the scheduler has not been able to address it. Perhaps it has been disconnected or it may simply be switched off. When it is re-enabled it will burst into life and print the file accounts-456 for the user **marion**.

The final part of the display lists the jobs, or spool files, awaiting printing. The four columns list the job number, the owner, the size of the spool file and the time it entered the queue. It is also possible to remove a job from the queue by typing:

```
$ cancel accounts-456
```

The example above assumes that you have identified this job number as the one you want to cancel by noting the output from lpstat -t. You can only cancel print jobs on files owned by yourself.

Troubleshooting   If **lp** does not appear to work, there could be a number of reasons:

1 The printer is not on line, out of paper, or not switched on.

2 **lp** is not supported on your system. For instance IBM AIX uses the command **print**.

3 The scheduler is not running. Type **lpstat -t** to see if this is the case.

4 The printer is not enabled. The scheduler gives each printer a logical name like 'gen'. **lpstat** may report that *gen* is not enabled in which case you could try the command

```
$ enable gen
```

Activity 19.4   Formatting print files

If you need to organise a report into a set number of lines per page, characters per line and so on, you could use the print preparation command **pr**.
The syntax of the command is **pr -options [file1]** ...

Output is to standard output which can be redirected to a printer or piped to the scheduler. **pr** does not itself cause printing to occur. Each page is separated by a heading containing the page number date and time and the name of the file.
The following are useful options switches:

-h 'text'	text in quotes following -h is output as a page header.
-l*n* where *n* is	the number of lines per page. (default=66)
-*n*	n column output, e.g. -3 for three column output
-o*n* where *n* is	the number of spaces in the left margin.
-t	suppresses the page number, date and time
-w*n* where *n* is	the page width

Options can be combined, e.g.

```
pr -h "Sales Report"  -l60 -o10 -w79 sales.rpt >/dev/tty8
```

This will cause the file **sales.rpt** to be output for printing with the heading 'May Sales Report' on each page. The report will have 60 lines to the page, have a left margin of ten characters and extend to 79 characters across the page.

Key words	cp
	cancel
	enable
	lp
	lpstat
	print queue
	scheduler
	serial port
	spool file

Section D: File and data processing utilities ■

UNIX provides some powerful tools for processing the data stored in standard ASCII type text files.

There are many sophisticated and often expensive packages available on most UNIX systems. Examples include database management systems and spreadsheets, as well as specific applications like stock control. But surprisingly effective, simple routine applications can be developed using shell commands. You will learn some of these techniques before assembling them into shell script programs.

Task 20 — Displaying part of a file

Objective

To investigate some of the commands individually in this section before putting them together into programs as illustrated in Section F.

Activity 20.1

Displaying the top of the file

It can be useful to inspect the first few lines of a long report or listing. The command head displays the first ten lines of a readable file, or as many lines as you specify:

```
$ head /etc/inittab
```

```
$ head +5 /etc/passwd
```

To make a change from inspecting the directories inittab and passwd, ask the system administrator to make a directory called **/ascii** to contain a number of ASCII type files of various lengths that you can use.

Activity 20.2

Looking at the end of a file

Certain files that are regularly updated with information recording or logging events or transactions are quite common in most computer systems. It is very convenient to be able to inspect the last few lines of such a file to see details of the most recent entries. The two examples below show you how to use the command. You will need to pick your own files to **head** and **tail**.

```
$ tail /ascii/icl.log
```
— displays the last 10 lines

```
$ tail +15 /ascii/spool.nl.85
```
— displays the last 15 lines

Task 21   Searching for patterns

Objective   To select lines from a file or display that match a condition or pattern.

Instructions   The filter **grep** takes its input from another command such as **ls** or from a file and outputs any line or lines that contain a string of characters supplied as a parameter.

Activity 21.1   Selective output from a command such as **ls**

```
$ ls -l ¦ grep Nov
```

In this example, output from **ls** is piped into **grep** which displays only those lines of the listing that contain the specified pattern. The effect is to restrict the listing to those files which were last updated in November. Try other months if you did not get a result for November.

   Now try the command substituting various patterns into the parameter after **grep**. After trying my examples below, make up some of your own.

```
$ ls -l ¦ grep rw-
```
— looks for files with rw- permission

```
$ ls -l / ¦ grep root
```
— looks for files in the root directory belonging to the root user

you could use grep to see if a particular user is logged on, e.g:

```
$ who ¦ grep joe
$ who ¦ grep tty5
```
(or some tty number within the range)

Activity 21.2   Searching a file for a pattern

In the examples above, **grep** took its input from a command. You can use **grep** to search a file for a pattern like this:

```
$ grep Susan phone.list
```
— displays lines in **phone.list** containing 'Susan'

```
$ grep root /etc/passwd
```
— displays the line in the **passwd** file containing 'root'

The general form of the command (the optional bits are shown in square brackets) is:

```
[input ¦]grep [switch(es)] pattern [file]
```

grep can take its input *either* piped from a command, which you substitute for [input], *or* it can operate directly on a file which you specify in place of the option [file].

Activity 21.3 Using some of the optional switches

The command can be refined by adding optional switches:

–i   case insensitive; **grep** would try to find Fred fred or FRED

–n   each matching line is displayed preceded by its relative line number in the file

–v   displays those lines which do *not* contain the specified pattern

```
$ grep -i turn phone.list
```

e.g.   `Michael Turnbull:302:405:Purchasing`

```
$ grep -in person  phone.list
```

The following example should list only those files in the root directory that do *not* belong to **root**:

```
$ ls -l / ¦ grep -v root
```

If the pattern to be searched contains metacharacters or spaces you will need to enclose the string in quotes:

Compare the effect of these two similar parameters:

```
$ ls -l ¦ grep 2
```

```
$ ls -l ¦ grep ' 2 '
```

The first example displays every line with a 2 in it.
The second example will display only those lines where the number 2 is not joined to other characters.

Activity 21.4   Further exercises

How would you display a listing of directories only? If you were to type

```
$ ls -l | grep d
```

you would get a list of directories under the root directory. The command would also display all those lines containing the letter **d** anywhere in the listing.

Since the owner of a directory is likely to have both read and write permission on their directory, you could use this to select directories with confidence:

```
$ ls -l | grep drw
```

As this is a useful utility, you can use **cat** to save it in a file that can be used as a shell *macro* command:

```
$ cat > lsdir (Return ↵)
ls -l | grep drw (Return ↵)
(Ctrl)+(d)
```

```
$ chmod +x lsdir
```

All you need to do now to list directories is to type the command:

```
$ lsdir
```

You will refine the command and make it available across the file tree in a later task.
    Work out how to display a listing of those files with the permission flags set to the pattern **-rw-rw-rw-** (answer on p. 110).

Key word   **grep**
              macro
              pattern

Task 22   Counting words and lines

Objectives

To count the number of words and lines in a file.
To add line numbers to a file.

Instructions

When you create a document or text file it is often useful to know how many words, lines or even characters there are in it.

You have seen from the example file **phones.list** that files can easily be constructed to contain records. Counting records is a database function that you will certainly require if you develop simple database applications using shell scripts. Commands such as **grep** and **wc** can be piped together to count those lines or records that match a certain pattern.

Activity 22.1

Counting the words and lines in various files

```
        $ wc phone.list
e.g.   4    20    105
```

The output in the example above means that there are four lines, twenty words and 105 characters in the file.

There are three optional switches that allow you to limit the output. The general form of the command is therefore:

```
wc [-clw] file(s)
```

  -c   display a count of characters only

  -1   display the number of lines only

  -w   display the number of words

More examples:

```
$ wc /etc/inittab
```

How many files in the root directory do not belong to the user **root**?

```
$ ls -l / ¦ grep -v root ¦ wc -l
```

In the above example, the output of **ls –l** is piped into **grep** using the **-v** switch which displays any lines that do not contain the parameter 'root'; the output of that is piped into **wc –l** which counts lines only.

Further practice:

1 Work out how many files in the root directory contain the permission string **-rw-rw-rw-** (answer on p. 110).

2 How many occurrences of the word **respawn** are there in the **/etc/inittab** file?

Activity 22.2   Adding line numbers to a display or file

When it is necessary to have line numbers added to a display or file you can use the command **nl**

```
$ nl /etc/inittab

$ nl phone.list > phone.num

$ cat phone.num
```

Warning: **nl** and **ln**

The obvious mnemonic for line-number is ln, but **ln** is the command that links a single file to other files or directories (*see* Task 16).

Key words   wc
                 -v
                 nl

Task 23

Rearranging file structures

Objectives

To display specified columns of a file.
To paste columns together from several files.
To switch the order of the columns of a file.

Instructions

Many applications organise data in the form of a table. Each column of such a table corresponds to a field and each row of the table corresponds to a record. The simple file **phone.list** has the form of a table.

In order to differentiate one column from another it is necessary to use a separating character, or **field delimiter**. In the case of phone.list tab stops were used as the delimiters to distinguish the columns. When the fields are likely to be of different lengths it is easier to use a delimiting character such as the colon.

Activity 23.1

Displaying selected columns of the passwd file

```
$ more /etc/passwd
```
— use pg if your system does not support more

```
$ more /etc/inittab
```

You can see that both these files use the colon as the field delimiter.
The fields of the passwd file are structured like this:

```
1   2                3   4   5        6           7
joe:odX4phsLq0z:200:208:joe short:/user/joe:/bin/sh
```

1 the user's id

2 the encrypted password

3 the user's number

4 the user's group number

5 optional field for notes about the user

6 the user's home or login directory

7 the user's shell

To display the list of users and their notes you need to cut fields 1 and 5 out of the file:

```
$ cut -f1,5 -d: /etc/passwd
```

Explanation	The **-f** switch specifies the fields you want to display while the **-d** switch defines the delimiting character. In this case **-d:** means the colon is the character that separates each field.

If you do not specify a delimiter, **cut** will assume that you have used tab stops or white space to separate the columns.

Activity 23.2	Displaying specified columns in your phone.list file and other functions.

```
$ cd;pwd
```

To display the Name column of the table only:

```
$ cut -f1   phone.list
```

To display Names *and* telephone extensions:

```
$ cut -f1,5 phone.list
```

Try out the above commands on the version of phone.list that you made before changing the delimiters to colons. You should have saved that version as phone.old

---

Activity 23.3	Making two more example files to illustrate the **paste** command

Sometimes you need to join the columns belonging to two or more files together vertically to make a new display or file.

To illustrate this technique, make the following files using **cat** or **vi**:

```
$ cat > list1
Allenby
Driscal
Fitches
Krishna
O'Hagan
Ctrl+d

$ cat > list2
200
350
120
480
500
Ctrl+d
```

You can paste the two files together to make a two column display:

```
$ paste list1 list2
```

Note that by default, **paste** sends its output to the screen (standard output) unless you redirect it elsewhere.
To make a new file consisting of two columns:

```
$ paste list1 list2 >list3
```

```
$ cat list3
```

Activity 23.4

Using both **cut** & **paste** to change the order of the columns of a table

```
$ cat phone.list
Name:Room:Ext:Dept
Michael Turnbull:302:405:Purchasing
etc.
```

If you would prefer to have the table organised like this:

```
Name:Dept:Room:Ext
Michael Turnbull:Purchasing:302:405
```

then you should follow steps 1–4 below.

1 Use **cut** to isolate the Dept column and save it to a temporary file called **dept.temp**

```
$ cut -f4 phone.list >dept.temp
```

```
$ cat dept.temp
```

2 Now **cut** out the Room and Ext columns and redirect them to another temporary file called **room.temp**

```
$ cut -f2,3 phone.list >room.temp
```

```
$ cat room.temp
```

3 Cut out the Name column:

```
$ cut -f1 phone.list > name.temp
```

You should now have three temporary files containing the columns Name, Room and Extension, Department. You can now use the command **paste** to stick them back together in the required order.

```
4  $ paste name.temp dept.temp room.temp
```

This will display the columns to standard output. To write the display to a file you must redirect the output to the new file:

```
$ paste name.temp dept.temp room.temp >phone.new
```

```
$ cat phone.new
```

You should now remove the temporary files:

```
$ ls-l *.temp                              (check that these are the
                                            ones to remove)
$ rm *.temp
```

Now reorganise phone.list so that the columns are in the following order: Department:Name:Room:Ext

Instructions

Summary of **cut** and **paste** options:

cut -c*list* — the numbers you supply as *list* define the absolute character positions to be cut out, e.g: **-c10–50** would cut out characters from position 10 to 50 all through the file.

cut -d*char* — specifies the list of fields to be cut out. e.g: **-f1,5** specifies fields 1 and 5, **-f3–5** specifies fields 3 to 5 inclusive.

cut -f*list* — specifies the list of fields to be cut out. e.g: **-f1,5** specifies fields 1 and 5, **-f3–5** specifies fields 3 to 5 inclusive

cut -s — suppress processing of lines with no delimiters.

paste reads its input from the list of files that you specify on the command line and joins them together vertically. Unless you specify a delimiter, **paste** uses tabs to separate the columns. The resulting lines are written to standard output or can be redirected elsewhere in the usual way.

Optional switches:

paste -d*list* — you can specify one or more delimiting characters

paste -s — serial merging of subsequent lines in the input file

Key words   -f
                        -d
                        cut
                        paste

Task 24   Sorting a file

Objective   To sort a file or files on various fields.

Instructions   Sorting data into numerical, alphabetical or date order is one of the most common data processing functions.

 sort takes data from standard input piped in from another command, or more usually, from a file or files. It sorts that data according to optional settings that control the sort criteria such as alphabetical, dictionary or numeric order. Data is sorted on a line by line basis unless a **key field** is specified.

Activity 24.1   Sorting by default

If no options are specified, **sort** will compar the characters in each position in every line of the file, including spaces, numbers, metacharaters, punctuation marks and so on. The sort is done in ASCII sequence which means that characters such as !"£$%^&* come before the numbers [0–9] which come before the letters A–Z. Following this are characters such as :;<=>?@ and finally lower-case letters [a–z].

 First try sorting the phone.list:

```
$ sort phone.list
```

You will see there is a problem in that the heading has become 'buried' in the middle of the file. To get around this problem, insert an asterisk in front of the word *Name* in the header column. You will have to use vi to do this.

```
$ vi phone.list
```

To insert ✶ in front of *Name*, position the cursor on the **N** of Name, press **i** for insert then type the asterisk ✶. Press the escape key **ESC**, then **:x** **ENTER** to save and exit from **vi**.

 Try sorting the file again. This time the header should stay at the top.

 Now go into **vi** again and change the name Wilkinson to WILKINSON, then sort the file once again. WILKINSON will go to the top because of the ASCII character sequence used by default.

 If you use the **-f** flag, **sort** will ignore upper and lower case differences and will put WILKINSON in its place:

```
$ sort -f phone.list
```

Activity 24.2   Sorting on different fields or columns

There is another problem which you may have noticed. Because the names have been entered in the format **Firstname Surname** e.g. Michael Turnbull, they will be sorted on first names rather than on surnames. If you do not specify a delimiter character using the **-t** switch, sort will assume that the delimiter is a space. Since there is a space between first name and last name you can use this to sort on the second column of the file even though you are using the colon as the 'official' delimiter:

```
$ sort +1 phone.list
```

This sorts on the first column after the first space, so you should get a sorted list based on the surnames in the second column.
Now sort the passwd file:

```
$ sort /etc/passwd ¦ more
```

The file should appear in user id order. Next try sorting on the user's number, which is the third field:

```
$ sort -t: +2 /etc/passwd ¦ more
```

-t: will define the column separator as the colon while **+2** means two columns *after* the first colon. In comparison with the usual elegant logic of UNIX commands this is rather confusing!
Look carefully at the output. You did not tell sort that this was to be a numeric sort so the order will not necessarily come out according to arithmetical values. This is a *character* sort which compares each character from left to right, thus 1000 will come before 200 and 23 will come before 9.

```
$ sort -t: +2 -n /etc/passwd ¦ more
```

Instructions   Some of the optional switches used with **sort**

-b   ignores blanks, white spaces, tabs

-d   dictionary order; considers letters, digits and blanks only

-f   ignores precedence otherwise taken by upper case letters

-n   sorts in numeric order

-o   directs the output to a file instead of to standard output. The file can be the same as the input file.

-r   reverse order; z–a or 9–0

-t   specifies field delimiter, e.g. t:

+n   defines the key field, e.g +2 is the second field *after* the first delimiter character.

Activity 24.3   Further practice

1 Experiment with phone.list, sorting it on different fields.
    Compare the result of sorting on the *Telephone Extension* field with and without the **-n** switch. Try out different combinations of switches. One thing you will find out is that it is not a good idea to include a table heading or title in the table itself!

2 Prepare three files containing lists of un-ordered dates. The file date1 should be in the format dd:mm:yy, date2 is in the American format mm:dd:yy, and date3 is in the format yy:mm:dd.

e.g:	*date1*	*date2*	*date3*
Date	dd:mm:yy	mm:dd:yy	yy:mm:dd
1st Nov 1989	01:11:89	11:01:89	89:11:01
29th Apr 1932	29:04:32	04:29:32	32:04:29
15th Dec 1950	15:12:50	12:15:50	50:12:15
	etc	etc	etc

Use your knowledge of **sort** to attempt to order each list in both ascending and descending order of dates. Remember: you can regard the ':' as a field separator.

Key words   sort
                       -t

Task 25   **Checking the differences between files**

Objectives

To spot the differences between versions of a file.
To change characters to a different case.
To spot duplicate lines within a file.

Instructions

The two commands **cmp** and **diff** can be used to report on the differences between two or more versions of a file. You can use **ls -l** to check the byte size of files and the date of the last update. This will give you a clue as to whether two versions of a file are different. To find out what the differences are, you need to use these more specialised utilities.

Activity 25.1

Using the **cmp** utility

cmp compares two files and reports the first difference that it finds. For example:

```
$ cmp phone.list phone.old
```

e.g. `phone.list phone.old differ: char 1, line 1`

Test this for yourself by making another copy of phone.list and then making a change to the new version and comparing the two.

Add some new lines to phone.list and then compare it with phone.old. You should get the message:

```
cmp: EOF on phone.old
```

This means that the End-of-File was discovered on phone.old before that on phone.list, which has the extra lines you have just added.

When processing files in a shell script you may not want the output of **cmp**, meagre as it is, displayed on standard output. The **-s** switch suppresses output and enables the use of the command within a file processing program, e.g.

```
if cmp -s file1 file2
then
```

(perform some action appropriate to there being no difference between file1 and file2)

```
else
```

(perform alternative action appropriate to file1 and file2 being different)

```
elif
```

Activity 25.2   Reporting differences in more detail

Try substituting the command **diff** for the command **cmp** in the examples above.
You will find that **diff** echoes the different lines from each of the two files, e.g.

```
$ diff phone.list phone.old
```

e.g.   1c1   < Name:Room:Ext:Dept

                    > *Name:Room:Ext:Dept

   This output shows that there is a small difference between the corresponding lines
of the two files: the second file has an asterisk before the word **Name**.
   Where one file has additional lines, instead of the rather terse 'EOF on phone.old',
they are echoed to standard output so that you can see exactly what they are. This
can be useful, or unnecessarily verbose; the point is that UNIX offers you the
opportunity to select the command that is most suited to your particular needs.

Activity 25.3   Trading cases

The **tr** command translates or *folds* characters from one case to another throughout
a whole file. In fact **tr** takes standard input, translates it according to a rule and
sends the result to standard output. You could use **tr** instead of **cat** to write a
message into a file.

```
$ tr '[a-z]' '[A-Z]' >test.caps
this is a message
Ctrl+d

$ cat test.caps
THIS IS A MESSAGE

$ tr '[A-Z]' '[a-z]'< test.caps >test.lower
$ cat test.lower
this is a message
```

Note that the two redirection symbols < and > cause **tr** to take its input from
test.caps while the output is redirected to test.lower.

Tidy up the temporary files:

```
$ ls test* test.caps test.lower
$ rm test*
```

Application: **tr** can be used in a shell script database application to force data entry
to uppercase characters if they are required in a given field.

Activity 25.4	Testing for duplicate records

In database applications it is an absolute necessity to be able to test a file to see if there are duplicate entries. In a given table each row or record should be unique.

In order for duplicate lines to be spotted they have to be next to each other. What file processing would you have to perform to ensure that this was the case? (Answer on p. 110)

First you must set up the Activity:

1 Make a copy of phone.list and call it phone.tmp

2 Create some duplicate lines by selecting them using **grep** and then redirecting the output to the end of phone.tmp

3 Sort the file, not just to standard output, but to itself.

4 Display the file to see that the duplicate lines are next to each other.

Try to do this for yourself; you have covered all the commands you need in order to perform these tasks.

You should now have a file with some duplicate lines. If not, follow the instructions on p. 110.

Now type the command:

```
$ uniq phone.tmp
```

This will remove the duplicated lines and any blank lines.
A new file consisting of unique records can be made by redirection:

```
$ uniq phone.tmp >phone.new
$ cat phone.new
```

Optional switches:

-c	counts the number of occurrences of each repeated line
-d	displays repeated lines only
-u	displays non-repeated lines only
-num	e.g. −3 skips over the first two fields
+num	e.g. +12 skips the first 12 characters

Key words   cmp
                       diff
                       tr
                       uniq

Task 26

Relational files

Objective

To join records from two files using a relational link.

Instructions

Complex databases are more often constructed from a set of related files or tables than from a single table. A common field or column acts as the link or relation between one or more tables. This organisation is particularly necessary when a number of transactions or events are associated with a single record in the master table.

   In the following example, each row in the master table holds data about a showjumping rider. Secondary tables track the progress of the riders in various shows. Another related table would record details of the horses.

   You can show the relationships between the tables by means of an **entity diagram** e.g.

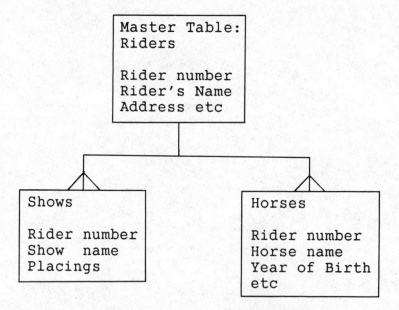

For each unique record for a rider there could be any number of results recorded in the shows table. A rider could also jump several different horses during a season.

   One problem with the rather simple arrangement above is that there is no way of recording which horse the rider rode in the shows table. If you have done some previous work on database design you might like to improve on this.

Activity 26.1   Setting up the files

For the sake of simplicity, you will work with only a rider table and a horse table, each containing the minimum necessary data.

Use **vi** or **cat** to make up the two tables:

```
$ cat >riders
120 Smith, S
105 Skelton, N
107 Whitaker, J
128 Broome, D
140 Edgar, M
103 Whitaker, M
etc
Ctrl+d

$ cat>horses
103 Henderson Didi
128 Lanegan
107 Henderson Milton
120 Brook Street Silver
140 Everest Unique
105 Alanpaul Apollo
etc
Ctrl+d
```

Activity 26.2   Joining the tables

Since the first field containing the rider number forms the *relation* between the two tables, both files must be sorted on that field:

```
$ sort -o -n riders riders

$ sort -o -n horses horses
```

Now you can use **join**:

```
$ join riders horses
```

Add some more records to the riders file:

```
cat >>riders
137 Pyrah, M
122 Hunter, J
```

Sort the riders file then do the join again. Only horses with corresponding riders will be displayed unless you use the **-a** switch.

−a1 displays lines in file1 not related to file2
−a2 displays lines in file2 not related to file1

```
$ join -a1 riders horses
```

To illustrate the possibility of a rider entering two horses in one event, add some more records to the horses table:

```
$ cat >>horses
103 Henderson Monsanta
105 Phoenix Park
140 Everest Sure Thing
```

Sort the horses file, then join the files again:

```
$ sort -o -n horses horses
$ join riders horses
```

The display should list all rides for each competitor. To list only, for example, the Whitaker brothers' horses:

```
        $ join riders horses ¦ grep Whit
e.g.    103 Whitaker, M  Henderson Didi
        103 Whitaker, M  Henderson Monsanta
        107 Whitaker, J  Henderson Milton
```

You should be beginning to see how powerful these commands can be in combination. Without the overhead of running a database management system, you are already beginning to process relational database tables, *without even having to do any programming!*

Joining other relational fields

You may wish to explore the possibilities of relational tables further. Once you start to develop the tables you will find that colon field delimiters are essential.

Consider these two tables:

1 The Horses table now has three columns:

```
rider_number:horse_number:horse_name

103:500:Henderson Didi
128:503:Lanegan
107:513:Henderson Milton
120:528:Brook Street Silver
140:533:Everest Unique
105:537:Alanpaul Apollo
103:546:Henderson Monsanta
105:547:Phoenix Park
140:560:Everest Sure Thing
```

2 The Results table has four columns:

```
Show name:rider_number:horse_number:placings

Royal Windsor:120:528:3,5,12
Dublin:105:537:8,1
HOYS:107:513:2,3,1
Royal Windsor:128:503:4
Dublin:105:547:3,11
HOYS:140:533:2,6
```

(HOYS = Horse of the Year Show)

If you wish to develop your skill at processing relational database tables in UNIX, you will need to edit the riders and horses files so that the column delimiters are colons. You will also need to set up the results file as shown above.

After joining, the final result should look like this:

```
File1_____   File2_____
Alanpaul Apollo:Dublin:8,1
```

i.e. you require the horse's name only from *Horses*, followed by the name of the show and the placings from *Results*.

Which column from each of the two files forms the relational link?

Answer: **file1 column2** links **file2 column3** by the common horse_number.

The steps that have to be carried out are:

1 sort file1 (horses) on col2

2 sort file2 (results) on col3

3 join the files using the following command:

```
join -t: -j1 2 -j2 3 -o 1.3 2.1 2.4 horses results
```

`-t:`   means use the colon delimiter

`-j1 2 -j2 3`   means **join** files by linking file1 col2 to file2 col3

`-o 1.3 2.1 2.4`   means output file1 col3, file2 col1, file2 col4

Rather complex commands like this one are usually put into a shell script so that you do not have to figure out the detailed use of the option switches every time.

Now try to create a list in the following format:

```
Alanpaul Apollo:Dublin:8,1:Skelton, N
```
etc.

This is the same as the previous example, with the rider's name added.

You will need to do the join as you did before except that you will need to output the first column from file1 (Horses). The output from this version of **join** must be redirected to another file; call it **results.tmp**

Then all you need to do is join **results.tmp** to **riders** and output the required columns. Work it out on paper first. Only look at p. 111 if you really cannot do it.

Key word	join

Section E: Introduction to programming in UNIX

Task 27   Simple shell macros

Objective

To construct one-line shell programs or 'macros'.

Instructions

The print formatting command at the end of Task 26 included several optional switches as well as a redirection to a device file. All this made the command rather unwieldy. It also increased the likelihood of you making a mistake or forgetting the exact syntax.

If you always need to print out the monthly sales report using the same standard format on the same printer, you can include the command in a simple one-line shell script, or **macro**. This could be called **prpt**, short for print report, then, instead of having to remember the command syntax:

```
pr -h "May Sales Report"  -160 -o10 -w79 sales_May.rpt >/dev/tty8
```

you can simply type: **prpt May**

and the file sales_May.rpt will be pre-formatted and printed.

Then, for the June report, all you have to do is type: **prpt June**

Activity 27.1 gives an easy example to begin with.

Activity 27.1

Setting up a simple macro to extract the time from the **date** command:

e.g
```
$ date
Fri Jul 19 11.03 GMT 1990
```

The time consists of characters 12 to 16 of the date string, so you can use **cut** to extract the time from the date string.

```
$ date ¦ cut -c12-16
11:04
```

Put this into a macro by using **cat** to copy the command to a file:

```
$ cat >tim
date¦cut -c12-16>tim
Ctrl+d
```

Make the file executable by changing the permission flags to rwx.

```
$ chmod +x tim
```

Now you can run the macro by typing its name:

```
$ tim
11.08
```

To practise this make a command called **mth** that extracts the month and day, like Feb 12.

Instructions

Passing the parameter

The monthly report command on page 83 required a parameter corresponding to the month which the user typed in after the command, such as prpt May or prpt Dec. The **tim** macro required no parameter; it was programmed only to extract the time from the date string. Other commands may require several parameters.

Command parameters are therefore numbered and are identified by a dollar sign placed in front of them, e.g. $1, $2 etc.

(MS–DOS batch file programmers will recognise these as replaceable parameters %1, %2, etc.)

If you take the command:

```
pr -h "May Sales Report"  -l60 -o10 -w79 sales_May.rpt >/dev/tty8
```

If you were to substitute **$1** for the word **May** and put this into the file prpt:

```
pr -h "$1 Sales Report"  -l60 -o10 -w79 sales_$1.rpt >/dev/tty8
```

you could then type **prpt 1990**

and the UNIX shell would process the command:

```
pr -h "1990 Sales Report"  -l60 -o10 -w79 sales_1990.rpt >/dev/tty8
```

However, do not try the commands above unless you have a printer on tty8 and a file called sales_1990.rpt that needs printing!

Activity 27.2   A macro to look up a phone number

It would be convenient to be able to type in the command **phone fred** and see Fred's number displayed. This was discussed in Task 21 Activity 2 where you typed **grep Sue phone.list**

By replacing the *absolute* parameter **Sue** with the *variable* parameter **$1** and saving the command to the shell macro **phone** you can both generalise the command and make it simpler to use:

```
$ cat >phone
grep $1 phone.list
ctrl-d

$ chmod +x phone
```

Now type:

```
$ phone Purch
```

You should be able to list all those entries in the Purchasing department.

```
$ phone Fred
```

This will extract all lines which include 'Fred'. If there were entries for Fred Bloggs and for Fred Astaire, both lines would be displayed.

Now type **phone Fred Astaire**
You will still get both Freds listed because you are passing two parameters to **phone** and the second is simply ignored.

If you type **phone "Fred Astaire"**, you will get an error message:

```
grep: Can't open Astaire
```

This means that the double quotes are sending "Fred Astaire" as a single parameter to **phone** which is then passing two parameters to **grep** which is trying to open a file called Astaire to search for Fred in.

You therefore need to enclose **$1** in double quotes:

```
$ cat >phone
grep "$1" phone.list
Ctrl+d

$ phone "Fred Astaire"
```

Key words   absolute parameter
                   variable

Task 28   **Shell variables**

Objectives   To access shell variables.
             To set up user-defined variables.
             To do simple arithmetic on variables.

Instructions   It is possible to store data in memory using **variables** which can be thought of as user-defined labels that identify a particular chunk of memory.

Variable names must always begin with an upper-case or lower-case letter and may contain numbers and the underscore character. There are certain **system variables** which have special significance.

Activity 28.1   Investigating system variables

Type the command **set** to get a list of the current settings that determine your working UNIX environment. System variables are in capitals, such as:

HOME	/user/fred	— the user's home directory
PATH	.:/bin:/usr/bin	— the directories to be searched to find programs whose names are entered as commands
LOGNAME	fred	— the user's id
MAIL	/usr/mail/fred	— the user's mailbox
PS1	$	— the UNIX prompt
PS2	>	— the continuation prompt, to be used when a command extends beyond the first line.

You can use **echo** to display the contents of a variable:

e.g. `$ echo HOME`
`/user/accounts`

e.g. `$ echo LOGNAME`
`joe`

Activity 28.2   Assigning values to variables

To use your own shell variables you assign data to them using the equals sign. They do not have to be declared.

```
$ name=Claude

$ echo $name
Claude

$ name=Claude Greenhill
Greenhill: not found
```

To assign to a variable containing white space, it must be enclosed in quotes:

```
$ name='Claude Greenhill'
$ echo $name
Claude Greenhill
```

You have already seen that quotation marks are important to commands such as **echo** and **grep**. There are three different types of quotation mark and each means something quite different.

1 Single quotes: ' '   Preserve the literal meaning of all the characters within the string.

2 Double quotes: " "   Enable variable name substitution within the string

3 Backwards quotes   ` `   Enable command substitution within the string

The significance of these rules will become clear when you try out these examples:

```
1  $ x=pwd

2  $ echo x
   x

3  $ echo $x
   pwd

4  $ echo "The command $x prints the working directory"
   The command pwd prints the working directory

5  $ echo '$x is a shell variable'
   $x is a shell variable

6  $ echo `$x`
   /usr/joe
```

Notes:

1 the string **pwd** is assigned to the variable x

2 the character x is echoed to standard output

3 the contents of the variable x is echoed

4 a string of characters is echoed including the contents of the embedded variable

5 the string is quoted verbatim

6 the shell substituted the *command* **pwd** which printed the working directory.

You could look at number 6 another way:

```
        $ wd=`pwd`
        $ echo $wd
e.g:    /usr/joe
```

This demonstrates how to store the output of a command in a variable. Here is another example:

```
        $ today=`date`
        $ echo $today
e.g.    Fri Jul 19 11.03 GMT 1990
```

How would you store only the month and day in the variable?

(Check this in Task 27 Activity 27.1)

```
$ today=`date | cut -c5-10`
$ echo today
```

Now extract the year from **date** and store it in a variable you can call **year**.

Activity 28.3   Multi-line variables

```
$ list='ada  [Return ↵]
>apl  [Return ↵]
>basic  [Return ↵]
>c  [Return ↵]
>cobol  [Return ↵]
>fortran  [Return ↵]
>pascal'  [Return ↵]
$
```

What is the difference between typing:

```
$ echo $list
```
and
```
$ echo "$list"
```

Activity 28.4

Reading a list from a file into a variable

Make a file that contains a list:

```
$ ls >files
$ files=`cat files`
$ echo $files
```

The above example is confusing because the memory variable and the file are both called 'files'.

To read the names in the file phone.list into a variable called names:

```
$ cut -d: f1 phone.list

$ names=`cut -d: fi phone.list`
$ echo $names
$ echo "$names"
```

Now write the contents of a multiline variable to a file.

1 Construct a multi-line variable or use the example **list** above if it is still in memory.

2 **Echo** the variable and redirect the output to the file.

3 Test your work by **cat**enating the file.

All these examples demonstrate individual techniques that will come into their own in the context of larger shell script programs.

Activity 28.5 Reading data into variables in the context of a program

To set up a program asking a user to enter data which can be stored in a variable, use the **read** command:

```
$ cat > act5
echo "Please enter your name:\c"
read name
echo "Hello $name!"
Ctrl+d
```

When you run the program by typing **sh act5**, the dialogue should look like this:

```
Please enter your name:Elvis
Hello Elvis!
```

After running the program yourself and testing it with various names, try typing the command:

```
$ echo $name
```

The name will not be echoed. This is because the variable only exists during the lifetime of the program act5. As soon as the program ceases to be executed, the variable dies. You can **export** the variable into the shell so that it can be used by other programs. Edit act5 using **vi** so that it contains the following lines:

```
$ vi act5
export name
echo "Please enter your name:\c"
read name
echo "Hello $name!"
```

Now run the program again:

```
$ sh act5
Please enter your name:Luciano
Hello Luciano!


$ echo $name
Luciano
```

To call sub-programs from a master program that need to access common variables, use the **export** command to make the variables generally available.

Activity 28.6   Simple arithmetic on variables

The command **expr** can be used to evaluate arithmetical operations performed on shell variables having integer values:

Try the following:

```
$ x=4
$ y=12

$ echo '$x $y'

$ expr $x + $y

$ expr $x - $y

$ expr $y - $x

$ expr $y / $x

$ expr $x \* $y
```

Note that you have **escape** from the normal meaning of the asterisk, which is a metacharacter, by preceding the asterisk with an oblique, called the escape character.

To assign the result of a calculation to a variable, place the expression inside back quotes.

```
$ z = `expr $x \*100`

$ echo $z
```

Key words   variable
system variable
back quotes
catenate
export
expr
escape

Formatting and record selection

Objectives

To format data from a file.
To select records for processing.

Instructions

You have already discovered that a file can be separated into fields more effectively using the colon as the separator. This enables fields to have variable lengths, which is a very flexible way of storing data. However, the file looks rather untidy when it is displayed using a simple command such as **cat**.

To lose the colons from the display and to line up the fields into columns, use the command **awk**.

awk is not just a command, but a mini-programming language similar to the C programming language. The file handling implicit in everything awk does has already been pre-programmed, saving the equivalent of many lines of C.

Activity 29.1

Formatting fields into columns

In Task 25 Activity 25.3, you made the file results which consisted of four fields:

```
$ cat results

Royal Windsor:120:528:3,5,12
Dublin:105:537:8,1
HOYS:107:513:2,3,1
Royal Windsor:128:503:4
Dublin:105:547:3,11
HOYS:140:533:2,6
```

awk uses the C programming **printf** statement to produce formatted printing. Try it first, and then study the explanation that follows:

```
$ awk -F: '{ printf "%-15s \t%d \t%d \t%10s \n",$1,$2,$3,$4 }' results

Royal Windsor 120    528            3,5,12
Dublin        105    537               8,1
HOYS          107    513             2,3,1
Royal Windsor 128    503                 4
Dublin        105    547              3,11
HOYS          140    533               2,6
```

Here is the general syntax of the **awk** command as you have just used it:

```
awk [-option] 'program' file(s)
```

The option **-F:** tells awk that the field separator is the colon.

The program which is enclosed within single quotes ' ' can be made up of a number of different statements contained within **braces:** { }. In the example the **printf** statement was the only statement.

The **printf** statement:

e.g.　`{ printf "%-15s \t%d \t%d \t%10s \n",$1,$2,$3,$4 }`

The first part of the statement in double quotation marks sets out the formatting to be applied to each of the fields to be displayed.

The second part consists of a list of those fields, referred to as $1, $2, etc, in the order you require.

`%-15s`　means:　left justify a string within a space of fifteen characters

`\t%d`　leave a tab space, then print a denary (base 10) number
(▨ stops the letter 't' from being printed)

`\t%10s`　right justify a string in a space of ten characters

`\n`　start a new line

%s refers to a string of characters and %d refers to an integer.

If you want to format a number which has decimal places, the code is **%f** (for **floating point**).

You assign a particular width to a field by inserting its value between % and the formatting character s,d or f.

A minus sign placed in front of the number means left justify the data within the allocated space.

Activity 29.2　　Selecting records

awk opens a file and reads it serially, one line at a time. In the examples in Activity 29.1, no particular pattern was specified, so **awk** performed the print action for every line of the file.

By specifying a pattern, you can select only those lines that contain a certain string of characters:

```
$ awk  '/Royal/' results
Royal Windsor:120:528:3,5,12
Royal Windsor:128:503:4
```

If no action is specified, {print} is performed by default.

The same result could have been achieved more simply by the command:

```
$ grep Royal results
```

The advantage of record selection within **awk** comes when you want to perform formatting functions or other processing on the records you have selected. A string of characters placed between forward obliques ▐ / ▐ / is called a **regular expression**. Any occurrence of that pattern within a line will cause it to be selected. If you want to select records on the basis of data in a particular field, you can use a **matching operator** such as the equals signs:

```
$ awk -F: '$2 == 105' results
Dublin:105:537:8,1
Dublin:105:547:3,11
```

In this example, the second field is tested against the value 105, and two records are selected. Each numbered field is referred to as $1, $2, etc. $0 refers to all the fields that make a particular line. The default field separator is a space or tab, so you would have to specify the colon as the field separator with **-F:**

Two equals signs are used to make the comparison, so as to distinguish between:
comparison e.g. x==2 (does the value of x equal 2?) and
assignment e.g. x=2 (let x take the value 2)

The matching operators are:

```
==          equal to
!=          not equal to
>           greater than
<           less than
>=          greater than or equal to
<=          less than or equal to
```

Now investigate the output if you substitute the following matching operations in the command below:

```
'$1 == "HOYS" '
'$1 != "Dublin" '
'$2 == 107'
'$2 >120'
'($2 + $3) == 573'
'$4 == 3,11'
'$4 == "3,11" '

awk -F: '               '      results
```

Activity 29.3   Using the logical operators **and or** to create multiple conditions

To select a record from the results file that satisfies more than one condition, e.g. 'Dublin' and 537, awk uses the symbols & & (double ampersand) as the *and* operator:

```
$ awk -F: '$1 == "Dublin" && $3 == 537' results
```

To select records having rider number 105 *or* rider number 140, use the double ▊ ▊ (pipe symbol):

```
$ awk -F: '$2 == 105 || $2 == 140' results
```

Activity 29.4   Using awk variables

Programming languages allow the temporary storage of data in variables. You will define and use your own variables but first you should look at the special variables provided by **awk** itself. As in the case of shell system variables, **awk** variables are distinguished from user variables by being in capital letters. Values are automatically assigned to these variables during processing and the results can be used.

Some useful **awk** variables

FILENAME	stores	the name of the current input file
FS		the field separator (default is whitespace)
NF		the number of fields in the current record
NR		the number of the current input record

NR and NF are particularly useful in data processing.
  Examine the output from the following examples, using the phone.list file. Just to remind you, the file looks like this:

```
Michael Turnbull:302:405:Purchasing
Stephen Wilkinson:219:125:Security
Deborah Adams:308:322:Personnel
David Lee Scott:400:325:Personnel
```

1   awk '{print NR,$0}' phone.lst

2   awk '/Adams/ {print NR,$0}' phone.lst

3   awk '{print NF,$0}' phone.lst

4   awk -F: '{print NF,$0}' phone.lst

Notes:
1 Prints the record number before displaying the record.

2 Selects only those records containing the string 'Adams'.

3 Prints the number of fields separated by white space.

4 Prints the number of fields separated by the colon.

Add the following record to the file:

```
$ echo "Linda Willoughby:Personnel" >> phone.lst
```

Records having a particular number of fields can be selected using the NF variable:

```
$ awk -F: 'NF==2' phone.lst
```

Assuming that only the names field contains spaces, we could find anyone with a name consisting of more than two words:

```
$ awk 'NF>2' phone.lst
David Lee Scott:400:325:Personnel
```

Activity 29.5   Mixing text and data in printf statements

The following **awk** program scans the file for the string 'bull' and displays the message:

```
Michael Turnbull belongs to the Purchasing Department
```

The command line to achieve this is rather long, so you can split it up. Press the
[Return ↵] key where shown. The secondary prompt > will appear, telling you
that the command is continuing on a subsequent line.

```
$ awk -F: ' <ì [Return ↵]
> /bull/ {printf "%s of the %s Department\n",$1,$4} [Return ↵]
> ' phone.lst [Return ↵]
```

You will learn other ways of dealing with long **awk** commands at a later stage.

Key words	awk
	printf
	regular expression
	matching operator
	formatting string

Task 30

Data processing and arithmetic

Objectives

To produce reports from unformatted data files.
To create **awk** program files.

Instructions

You will now learn how to combine the powerful formatting commands you have
already learned with arithmetical and string functions.

You need a new data table which stores workers' names, their rates per hour and the
number of hours worked:

```
$ cat > pay
Ali 10 35
Bilton 8 40
Hardy 12 20
Jetha 8 30
Singh 12 40
Ctrl+d
```

Your finished report should look like this:

```
NAME        RATE       HRS        GROSS       TAX(25%)
Ali         10.00      35         350.00      87.50
Bilton       8.00      40         320.00      80.00
Hardy       12.00      20         240.00      60.00
Jetha        8.00      30         240.00      60.00
Singh       12.00      40         480.00     120.00
TOTALS                 165       1630.00     407.50
```

Activity 30.1

Performing arithmetic

Start by doing the arithmetic needed to produce the GROSS and TAX

```
$ awk '{print $1,$2,$3,$2*$3,$2*$3*.25}' pay
```

Notice that you can use the arithmetical operators + − * / on existing columns to
produce new columns. To format the result correctly you will need to define columns
2, 4 and 5 as floating point decimal numbers with two places. Here are some
examples of floating point formatting strings:

%f	default floating point format
%6f	floating point number in a six digit field
%5.2f	2 decimal places in a five digit field
\t%.1f	1 decimal place after a tab space

The command will now be so long that it will spill over on to the next line. Type it in, pressing the (Return ↵) key where shown:

```
$ awk ' (Return ↵)
> {printf "%-10s \t%.2f \t%d \t%.2f \t%.2f\n", (Return ↵)
> $1,$2,$3,$2*$3,$2*$3*.25}' pay (Return ↵)
```

The command will get even longer when you include the column headings and the totals! When a program gets too long to go on one line, write it into a program file which awk can read.

First do the arithmetic that produces the totals. To add up all the numbers in a column, a variable is used to accumulate the total. Start by adding up all the hours in column 3:

```
$ awk '{hours = hours+$3} END {print hours}' pay
```

You can increment a variable using the C programming shorthand, so hours = hours+1 can be rendered hours += 1

The special pattern END causes subsequent actions to be performed *after* **awk** has scanned all the records.

Activity 30.2   Writing an awk program

The command line required to add up columns 3, 4 and 5 will be too long, so use **vi** to create an **awk** program file and call it rpt1.awk

```
$ vi rpt1.awk

{
    hours += $3
    gross += ($2*$3)
    tax   += ($2*$3*.25)
}

END { printf "TOTALS:\t\t%d \t%.2f \t%.2f \n", hours,gross,tax }
```

The conventions about how to use the braces ▐ ▌ are similar to those in C programming. Such conventions are not strictly necessary but they help to make the program more readable.

Run the program by embedding it in the following version of the **awk** syntax:

```
        awk -f program  datafile(s)
```

```
e.g:    $ awk -f rpt1.awk pay
```

The switch **-f** tells **awk** to read program instructions from an external command file instead of the command line. Do not confuse -f with the -F switch which defines the field separator. If you need to use the -F switch, it goes between the program and the datafile. If the file pay were delimited by colons you would type:

```
awk -f rpt1.awk -F: pay
```

Activity 30.3   Topping and tailing

To finish off the report, you need to print the headings at the beginning of the program, before **awk** starts to read through all the records.

   Actions which have to be executed before the file is read are associated with the pattern BEGIN. It is good practice to initialise variables to their starting values at this point; you can then see at a glance what variables are to be used during the program. Comments can be preceded by the **hash** sign #.

   Use **vi** to edit the program to the complete version:

```
$ vi rpt1.awk
```

Run the report by typing: `awk -f rpt1.awk -F: pay`

```awk
#  Awk program file: rpt1.awk
#  Source file: /usr/joe/pay

BEGIN  {
        hours = 0
        gross = 0
        tax   = 0

        print "NAME            RATE    HRS     TAX"
     }

{
  printf "%-10s \t%.2f \t%d \t%.2f \t%.2f \t%.2f \n",$1,$2,$3,$2*$3,$2*$3*.25
}

{
 hours += $3
 gross += ($2 * $3)
 tax   += ($2 * $3) * .25
}

END {
     printf "TOTALS: \t\t%d \t%.2f \t%.2f \n",hours,gross,tax
    }
```

Counting records

Often you need to know how many records there are in a file which satisfy some condition. For instance, you could count the number of records in the **passwd** file that do not have a password in the second field.

The **length** function can be used to test the length of a field. What we want **awk** to do is to look at each line of the **passwd** file and add one to a variable called *count* every time the length of the second field is equal to zero.

```
$ awk -F:'
> length($2) == 0 {count ++}
> END {print count "entries in the "FILENAME" file have no passwords"}
> ' /etc/passwd
```

Notice that you can increment a variable by adding one to it using the shorthand notation **count ++** which is the same as **count +=1** and **count = count + 1**. For the purpose of the example, the print statement references the **awk** variable FILENAME.

Key words	**floating point format**
	increment

Task 31   A shell program

Objective

To be able to write a menu program using **while** loops and **case** statements.

Instructions

A useful application you could develop is a program to log calls that might be made to a computer technical support company. A typical scenario might be:

You discover that your keyboard is not working correctly — the enter key keeps sticking. You type the command **fault** (which is the program you are about to write) and this gives you the support company's telephone number to call. When you get through, their operator will give you a fault number and ask for a brief description of the fault. The program will record the fault number, your initials, and the location of the faulty equipment. Finally you will type in a summary of the fault.

The program will write each fault record to a file which will look something like this:

```
TASK 31 A SHELL PROGRAM

DATE   TIME  NO  USR ROOM  SUMMARY
10 Jan 11.43 103 JS  12    Enter key sticks on terminal 12
11 Jan 14.51 104 GH  02    Laser printer o/s -Font cartridge faulty?
12 Jan 09.45 103 JS  12    Engineer replaced k/b; OK
12 Jan 10.00 104 GH  02    Font cartridge OK; took away printer
13 Jan 09.30 104 GH  02    Laser printer returned; OK
```

The fault logging program will require at least three options:

1 Display the fault log file

2 Add a fault record to the log

3 Search the log for record(s) that match a pattern

To make the program easy to use, a **menu** should be provided that indicates the available options.

Activity 31.1   Preparing the menu

Use **vi** to make a file called fault.menu

```
$ vi fault.menu
FAULT LOGGING PROGRAM

   Menu of Options

1  Display the fault log

2  Add a fault to the log

3  Search log by date, operator or other pattern

4  Return to UNIX
```

After using **vi** make sure that the menu looks right: `$ cat fault.menu`

Activity 31.2   The program skeleton

The menu, together with the program lines required to execute the options, are contained within a **loop**, so that the user is returned to the menu after using a particular option. In order to break out of the loop, the final or *n*th option must provide an exit route!

The UNIX statements that execute such a loop are quite simple:

```
while true

do

          (series of program statements, including exit – otherwise the
          loop will go on and on and on)

done
```

Inside the loop will be the program code which executes the choices. If you have done some programming before, you will probably have come across the CASE construction, which enables a series of choices to be processed.

Assuming that the choice number has already been read into a variable called choice, the **case** syntax is:

```
case $choice in
```

1   [command statements needed to execute choice 1]
   ;;
2   [command statements needed to execute choice 2]
   ;;

etc

```
n)
      echo Returning you to UNIX
      exit
      ;;

esac
```

Notes:
n is the last or nth choice which will enable you to exit from the **while** loop.

esac (which is **case** backwards) marks the end of the **case** construction. In UNIX, familiar programming constructions such as *if..endif* and *case...endcase* take the form:

if...fi *and* **case...esac**.

Statements associated with each choice are terminated by two semi-colons **; ;**

Activity 31.3   Writing the program

Use **vi** to edit the program. Do not include line numbers, as they are only for reference to explain certain points to you later on. See page 105.

```
1 # fault    -Fault logging program
2
3 while true
4 do
5
6    cat fault.menu
7    echo "Enter a number:\c"
8    read choice
9
10   case $choice in
11
12   1)  # display fault.log
13
14        echo "Date  Time Fault User    Comments"
15        echo "           No.   Initials
16        more | fault.log
17        echo "Press ENTER to continue...\c"
18        read continue
19        ;;
20
21   2)  # update fault.log
22
23        tail -5 fault.log    # displays the last five records
24        echo "Call tech support on 33256 and ask for a fault number"
25        echo "Enter your initials:\c"
26        read user
27        today = `date +"%d%h %H.%M"`
28        echo "Enter fault number:\c"
29        read "faultno"
30        echo "Enter room number where faulty device is located:\c"
31        read room
32        echo "Summary of fault:\c"
33        read summary
34
35        echo "$today:$faultno:$user:$room:$summary" >>fault.log
36        tail -5 fault.log
37        echo "Press ENTER to continue...\c"
38        read continue
39        ;;
40
41   3)  # search for selected records
42
43        echo To display selected lines only, please enter the pattern
44        echo you wish to match, such as a date, room, device name\n
45        echo "Type in the pattern:\c"
46        read match
47        grep $match fault.log | more
48        echo Press ENTER to continue...
49        read continue
50        ;;
51
```

```
52  4)   # exit from the loop and return to UNIX
53
54       echo Returning you to UNIX
55       exit
56       ;;
57
58    esac
59
60  done
```

Notes on the program

Line   Explanation

3   start of the while loop

6–8   display the menu and get the choice

10   start of the case construction

19   each case statement has to be ended with ;;

27   the date command has special formatting strings similar to those you have met in **awk:**

```
%d day in numerical form
%h Month in abbreviated form
%H Hours
%M Minutes
```

`date + "%d/%h %H:%M"` would generate a display like: 15/Oct 10:35

58   the case statement is terminated with **esac**

60   the **while...do** statement is terminated with **done**

Activity 31.4   Using the program

To test out the program you must make it executable:

```
$ chmod +x fault

$ fault
```

There are a number of additions and improvements that you could add. For example, you could use **awk** to produce a really smart, formatted report. Using **awk** you could also count the number of times certain categories of equipment go wrong, the number of days that the equipment is out of service, and so on.

Appendix 1

List of UNIX
commands
and their
functions

Appendix 2

Answers to selected problems

Task 8
Activity 8.2

`-r--r-----` = a file, read only, owner and group

`-rw-r--r--` = a file read/write for the owner; read only for everyone else

`drw-rw-r--` = a directory, read/write for owner and group; read only for others

`brwxrwxrwx` = a block device, probably a disk, with full access to all users

Task 9
Activity 9.3

To make the directories below cplus, type the command:

```
$ mkdir bin lib include sys apps

$ ls -l
```

Task 11
Activity 11.2

There are two passwd files: one is the program file that enables users to enter their passwords; the other is a data file that contains the list of passwords.

The program file, probably located in /bin, is an example of an executable binary file. The passwd data file lives in /etc and it consists of ASCII text and is human-readable. It contains a list of users and processes, their ids and passwords. The passwords are encrypted or scrambled so that you cannot read them.

Write permission on this file belongs to the system administrator or 'super-user'.

Task 14

Example 1 – renames the file **myfile.old** to **myfile**

Example 2 – moves all files ending with suffix **.old** to the directory **/oldfiles**

Example 3 – moves the list of two files to **/accounts**

Example 4 – renames the directory **dbs** to **database**

Example 5 – two files have been moved one after the other to a file called backup. Unless backup is a directory located immediately below the working directory, the file fault.log will overwrite the previous version of backup which was the file memo3.joe.

Task 14
Activity 14.1

To make dummy files:

```
$ touch ibmterm.old

$ touch nl.data sl.data pl.data
```
etc

To make the directory dbs, with the parent directory as your home directory:

```
$ cd

$ mkdir dbs oldfiles
```

Task 16

-rwxr-xr-x signifies that the owner has full read, write and execute permission over the file. Both the group and other users may read and execute the file only. This means that the owner can make changes to the file by writing to it, but others cannot. For a shell script to run, the shell needs to *read* the program in order to *execute* it.

Task 21
Activity 21.4

```
$ ls -l ¦ grep "-rw-rw-rw-"
```

Quotation marks are required because **-r** would otherwise be misinterpreted as a switch such as rm -r.

Task 22
Activity 22.1

1 To find out how many files in the root directory have permission flags set to rw-rw-rw-, you could type:

```
$ ls -l / ¦ grep -rw-rw-rw- |wc -l
```

2 To find the occurrences of the word respawn in /etc/inittab:

```
$ cat /etc/inittab ¦ grep respawn |wc -w
```

Task 25
Activity 25.4

To ensure that duplicate lines follow sequentially you need to sort the file. These are the steps to take in setting up the activity:

```
$ cp phone.list phone.tmp

$ grep t phone.list >>phone.tmp
```

This selects any record with a 't' in it and appends the records, using the double redirect symbol ▶ ▶, to the end of the file phone.tmp

```
$ sort -o phone.tmp phone.tmp
```

Task 29
Activity 29.2

```
$ echo "New Forest and Hampshire:120:528:5,2">>results
```
Alternatively, you could edit the file using **vi**.

Appendix 3 ▬▬▬▬▬▬▬▬

**How to fix a
hung terminal**

If a terminal 'hangs' or locks up on you, there will be an associated process running on the CPU which has to be terminated in order to break the deadlock. You need to know your user id and, if possible, the terminal id. You must then login at another terminal, using the same id as the one logged into the hung terminal.

Then use the command **ps** which reports on the currently running processes. The flags **-ef** give a full display, e.g.

```
$ ps -ef
```

UID	PID	PPID	STIME	TTY	COMMAND
root	0	0	Jan 1	?	[schedule]
root	1	0	Jul 23	?	/etc/init
root	2	1	Jul 23	?	[pagdemon]
root	3	1	Jul 23	?	[swapper]
root	21550	1	Jan 11	cons	/usr/lib/errdemon
lp	21546	1	Jan 11	?	/usr/lib/lpsched
tetra2	26398	1	12:58:38	7	-sh
fitchett	25928	1	17:01:34	3	-sh
tetra2	26411	26398	12:58:53	7	tmenu tetramenu
joe	26218	1	13:10:32	8	-sh
oracle	26027	1	07:58:09	15	bwrF
oracle	26028	1	07:58:12	15	biwF
oracle	26029	1	07:58:15	15	clnF
tetra2	26412	26411	13:01:48	7	n12 nlfenq
fitchett	26432	25928	17:01:48	3	sql
joe	26603	26218	13:11:45	8	/bin/csh
fitchett	26477	26432	17:01:51	3	oraclF P:4096,3,6
joe	26522	1	17:21:03	5	-sh
joe	26523	26522	17:21:47	5	ps -ef

The columns refer to user id, process id, parent process id, system time, and command. The first six entries relate to system processes, most of which have the initialisation program /etc/init as their parent process. Let us assume that user joe's terminal is the one that has hung. His login shell has the PID 26218 and the terminal is 8. The C shell was run and it has hung. Notice that joe has logged in on terminal 5 and that **ps -ef** reports on itself; this is always the last entry in the table.

If joe uses the command **kill -9** on process number 26603 it should clear the stuck cshell. If this does not work, joe could kill the parent process, that is PID 26218. This will log terminal 8 off the system, which is probably the best thing to do, e.g.

```
$ kill -9 26218
```

Whatever software package you are learning...

- dBase III+ ● Sage Book-keeper ● Multiplan
- Lotus 1-2-3 ● Ventura ● DataEase ● Pegasus
- SmartWare ● Aldus PageMaker ● SuperCalc 5
- Lotus 1–2–3 ● WordPerfect 5.1 ● WordStar ● Word
- Timeworks 1.3 ● Microsoft ● Quattro Pro 3
- Sage Accountant and Accountant Plus

You will find a book in the Pitman *Training Guide* series suited to your needs.

Each title follows the same, effective format:

- the text is fully comprehensive yet free of jargon
- instructions are carefully structured
- covers all the main functions of the package: loading, creating, quitting, locating, altering, storing etc
- tasks and exercises teach the various commands and reinforce learning

Ask for the titles in the *Training Guide* series in your local bookstore. Alternatively, contact our sales department:
Pitman Publishing, 128 Long Acre, London WC2E 9AN
Telephone: 071-379 7383